11-10

The Art
of Comforting

The Art
of Comforting

· ✦ ·

*What to Say and Do for
People in Distress*

· ✦ ·

Val Walker

Jeremy P. Tarcher/Penguin

a member of Penguin Group (USA) Inc.

New York

JEREMY P. TARCHER/PENGUIN
Published by the Penguin Group
Penguin Group (USA) Inc., 375 Hudson Street, New York, New York 10014, USA •
Penguin Group (Canada), 90 Eglinton Avenue East, Suite 700, Toronto, Ontario M4P 2Y3,
Canada (a division of Pearson Penguin Canada Inc.) • Penguin Books Ltd, 80 Strand,
London WC2R 0RL, England • Penguin Ireland, 25 St Stephen's Green, Dublin 2, Ireland
(a division of Penguin Books Ltd) • Penguin Group (Australia), 250 Camberwell Road,
Camberwell, Victoria 3124, Australia • (a division of Pearson Australia Group Pty Ltd) •
Penguin Books India Pvt Ltd, 11 Community Centre, Panchsheel Park, New Delhi–110 017,
India • Penguin Group (NZ), 67 Apollo Drive, Rosedale, North Shore 0632, New Zealand
(a division of Pearson New Zealand Ltd) • Penguin Books (South Africa) (Pty) Ltd,
24 Sturdee Avenue, Rosebank, Johannesburg 2196, South Africa

Penguin Books Ltd, Registered Offices: 80 Strand, London WC2R 0RL, England

Most Tarcher/Penguin books are available at special quantity discounts for bulk purchase
for sales promotions, premiums, fund-raising, and educational needs. Special books or book
excerpts also can be created to fit specific needs. For details, write Penguin Group (USA) Inc.
Special Markets, 375 Hudson Street, New York, NY 10014.

Library of Congress Cataloging-in-Publication Data

Walker, Val.
The art of comforting: what to say and do for people in distress / Val Walker.
       p.   cm.
ISBN 978-1-58542-828-1
1. Compassion.   I. Title.
BJ1475.W35   2010   2010024236
177'.7—dc22

Printed in the United States of America
1   3   5   7   9   10   8   6   4   2

Book design by Marysarah Quinn

Contents

Introduction

I T CAN BE A HARD WORLD to be soft in—to remove the Teflon we wear amid all the impatience and cynicism around us just to be there for someone who needs our love and support. Qualities like gentleness, patience, warmth, and empathy can be so undervalued in this day and age that when we need to sit down with someone devastated by a loss or turbulent change in their lives, we often feel unsure about what to say or do.

Given how uncomfortable the act of comforting can feel, many people completely avoid getting close to a distressed or grieving person. They either barely acknowledge or say nothing at all about what the person is going through. Others offer cheerful remarks or uplifting platitudes, such as "Something good will come out of this" or "God will show you the way." Still others drop off food, flowers, or gifts, only to disappear after a week or two. Yet the person in pain can feel as isolated by the smiling well-wishers as by the avoidant ones. Sometimes grieving people find it easier to just hide, thinking that, at least this way, they won't make others feel bad.

But highly comforting people still prevail, albeit quietly in the background and without much fanfare. And they have much to teach those of us who wish to restore the lost art of comforting into our lives.

I N THE FIRST BLEAK MONTHS after my divorce, I returned to my home state of Virginia after five years of following my husband's career moves to Minnesota and New Jersey. Heartbroken and homesick, traveling with my faithful, adaptable cat, Ivan, I imagined my homecoming would be wonderful and warm, surrounded by welcoming old friends, family, and colleagues.

To my surprise and dismay, people were disappointingly unforthcoming. I was not automatically invited to parties, dinners, reunions, and gatherings. I could hardly get folks to commit to a cup of coffee or to stop over to my modest apartment for a pasta salad. So busy with their own families, jobs, problems, and responsibilities, it seemed no one could squeeze me in for some "quality" time. But I was offered plenty of advice, platitudes, opinions, and cheer about how to move forward with my new life. "You're better off without him." "You need to find a singles support group." "Living well is the best revenge." My Christian friends told me to pray more, and my New Age friends chided me to meditate more. I should practice yoga, read self-help books, open up a savings account, travel, take flute lessons, stop seeking approval from others, tap into my playful inner child. When offered these tips to get over my grief, as if just being handed a brochure about my condition by a hurried doctor, I felt pushed away. Did anyone, besides a therapist or pastor, have the time, let alone the patience and interest, to sit down with me, to talk heart-to-heart? But God forbid anyone spot my neediness, or worse, my loneliness! So, for the purpose of maintaining my reputation as a likable, invitation-worthy person, I hid my hunger for comfort from people. I resorted to holding Ivan in my lap at night, with a box of tissues, popcorn, and Animal Planet on TV.

One day, Morna, an old friend from Scotland, phoned and asked if she could come visit me soon. She could take a week off from her psychotherapy practice and "really wanted" to see me. We hadn't met for years, and I had missed her terribly. I was ecstatic, but had to keep my neediness in check. I invited her to come in October, offering my foldout sofa bed and free home-cooked food.

When she arrived at my spruced-up apartment, we immediately opened a bottle of sherry and lit candles to celebrate. She gave me gifts, a beautiful green agate stone and a book of poems, and I entertained her with the latest movies, a fun itinerary of sights to see, and a show-and-tell of the pillows I had made for three chairs. We were off to a good start.

My neediness was kept buttoned-down fairly successfully for the next three days. Morna, with her impeccable Scottish manners and brisk humor, seemed quite happy with my fake-it-to-make-it strategy of performing as a gracious hostess. Certainly, after her effort to travel across the ocean to spend her precious time with me, she deserved the best of me and the best views of Virginia, with a drive through the Blue Ridge Mountains and a stroll in the gardens of Monticello. She gently asked how I was coping with being alone, but I assured her I was learning how to keep positive and busy. She offered me opportunities to open up and talk, but I didn't dare expose my neediness.

Finally, a year's worth of pent-up grief and despair erupted in my kitchen on Morna's fourth day with me. Fixing her an omelet and sausages for breakfast, I burned myself and dropped the frying pan full of grease all over the floor. I snapped, threw the spatula against the wall, slammed my fist on the cupboard, kicked sausages across the floor, and yelled a slew of profanities. I crawled down on the floor to wipe up the battered eggs and mess, and collapsed into tears.

"I'm such a loser!" I wailed. "I can't even fry eggs for you!"

Huddled on my knees, sobbing, I hadn't noticed that Morna had quietly approached me. She sat down on the kitchen floor next to me and softly put her hand on my shoulder.

I glanced at her quickly without making eye contact and said, "Now you see what a basket case I really am."

"I see someone who is in pain . . . a lot of pain."

I wept longer, letting her words sink in. She was right. I felt relief just hearing her say the truth out loud.

"Yes, that's right. I've been really, really hurt. I feel so alone. I am so afraid no one wants to be with me anymore."

Morna made herself more comfortable on the floor, sitting cross-legged. "I don't mind listening, if you want to talk about this now."

I remembered she was a professional counselor and blushed. "You sure you aren't just playing counselor with me? You're supposed to be getting a break from listening to people in pain all the time."

She smiled softly, and paused. "I'm your *friend*. Why do you think I'm sitting here on the floor with you?"

Feeling welcomed to speak from my heart, uncensored, I took the plunge to trust her. The floodgates opened. We sat on the kitchen floor for another hour, until our legs ached, then moved to the sofa and talked nonstop until 3 a.m. In the next day's storytelling marathon we cried, ranted, laughed, ate chocolates, threw toys for Ivan, and cursed at the lawyers, doctors, creditors, lovers, and in-laws who had screwed us over. By evening, my rip-roaring emotions felt purged well enough to suggest to Morna we go out for sushi.

Still, I soaked up some tears with my napkin over our dinner on our last night together, yet felt completely accepted and at ease.

In my last few minutes with her at the airport, as she was about to step past the gate for her plane, I repeatedly blurted out, "Morna, I can't thank you enough."

She paused and put down her suitcase.

I shrugged anxiously, "How can I ever repay you?"

She gave me a long, mighty hug, then looked boldly into my eyes. "You've already paid me back. You've given me your trust, after all the hurt you've been through. You've given me more than I ever dreamed of. Thank *you*."

Too moved to speak, I barely nodded and hugged her quickly one last time.

I watched her disappear into the crowds to board her plane, still filled with the warmth and tenderness she had bestowed upon me. As an ocean of people passed by me, I made my way through the maze of lobbies and escalators to my car.

Then, in the parking lot of Dulles Airport at rush hour, with roaring planes coming and going overhead, I paused to marvel at a blazing October sunset. Standing under a wild sky bursting with gold and crimson light, I realized I could bear my raw, unruly grief with acceptance and even love. Though I might never heal completely, as long as I could find comfort with at least one true friend, the beauty of the sky, and one old sweet cat, I was going to be okay.

A Rare Skill

Morna's visit provided me with the comfort I had been craving, but it also left me wondering why comforting people were so hard to find. And even if we do find those who are willing and ready, why is it so hard for people to just sit with someone who is suffering without trying to make their pain go away so they can just "get over it"?

Further, I knew that providers around me, including psychotherapists, pastoral counselors, nurses, physicians, yoga instructors, and other healers were not paid to simply comfort people like me in the rawest, most acute stages of grieving. Though knowledgeable and well trained, and often warm and caring, these professionals were paid to heal people, change people, treat people, and do this as efficiently as possible— to give us their "bang" for our buck. Of course, especially in America, where health care costs consumers so much of their hard-earned money, professionals were trained to fix us as quickly as possible. Not much time for sitting with us while we have a good cry or stare hopelessly at the walls trying to wrap our overwhelmed minds around scary things like our "future," or our "recovery," let alone our sky-high pile of bills. Like many people going through difficult times, I wasn't quite ready for healing yet—I needed comforting first and foremost. And the lack of available comforters made my grief twice as painful.

Morna offered me something that few professionals or laypeople are willing or even able to offer: She allowed me to fall apart in her presence. She didn't judge me, diagnose me, hire me or fire me, fix me, bill me, instruct me, save me, or heal me. She wasn't trying to be absolutely unconditionally loving or saintly. She wasn't even trying to make me smile. She just sat with me amid the mess in my kitchen, the mess in my life, and the mess in my heart and allowed me to be in my pain. Unfazed by all this mess, she sat there and held it all together with her mere presence.

Presence. Unshakable, steady, tender, and empathic presence. Soft strength. That was comfort. That was Morna's gift to me.

Think about what a cast or a brace does for a broken arm or leg. They hold the broken part of our body in place until that part can get strong and grow back again. They support and hold us together until we can stand up, or walk, or run again. A comforter's *em*brace does the same thing, holding us together when we feel broken. A comforter doesn't need anything from us, not even for us to heal or get better or get well. Something about Morna's peaceful and gentle acceptance of my vulnerability gave me the chance to *em*brace the fractured, shadow parts of myself. She saw the good, the bad, and the hidden parts of me. Then, with nothing to hide, nothing to cover up or make up, I said nothing and she said nothing. This *nothing* moment of sitting on the kitchen floor in the mess changed my life.

Writing the Book I Couldn't Find

Later, after I'd grown a little stronger, I moved from Virginia to Maine. At first I envisioned Maine as a temporary respite, a place to live for a couple of years while I reinvented my life. Coastal Maine, Vacationland, was safe, rural, and quiet enough for me to heal, away from the din and drama of the bigger cities I had once thrived in as I pushed myself hard for upward mobility, along with my highly ambitious husband. Finally, I could slow down, soften, and find my inner voice, sitting on sun-soaked mossy rocks beside rivers and bays watching blue herons, egrets, and ospreys.

But Maine grew on me, and I've stayed here. I made new friends and discovered a genuine, unique community in the town of Yarmouth, where I settled for good. I found peace, my own serene providence on the rocky coast near a colony of blue herons, one of the largest sanctuaries for herons in New England. On some summer mornings, I can see as many as eighteen herons standing still at low tide, silhouetted against the sunrise.

I eventually took a job as a bereavement coordinator for a hospice in 2004. I had previously worked as a rehabilitation counselor at a hospital in Richmond, Virginia, serving cancer patients and their families, as well as rehab programs with Veterans Affairs clients and other groups of people in turbulent stages of their lives. Since 1992, I had specialized in facilitating support groups for issues such as grief and bereavement, coping with chronic illness, job loss, and other kinds of loss, such as loss of a home, or bankruptcy. I enthusiastically launched a popular training course for facilitators of grief support groups in Bridgton, Maine, and later, as a consultant, provided training for support group facilitators throughout Maine.

My rehabilitation counseling background had offered rich opportunities to learn the art of comforting with a wide range of groups, but in particular I learned from the group participants *themselves* who told me what specifically comforted them. I was heartened to realize that what I had felt from Morna's comfort was very similar to what others had felt when truly comforted. There were common threads of

comforting, certain words, actions, and gestures that people cherished from comforters who kindly and patiently
stepped into their lives. In dozens and dozens of support
groups, people told me the same things about comforters. But
why was this practical wisdom about the art of comforting
not common knowledge? Even individuals whose professions
directly or indirectly seemed to require comforting skills
appeared to lack them. Maybe we saw some of them in our
health care, pastoral care, and psychiatric services, or in
human services and social work fields. Too many experts did
not have the basic comforting skills generously exhibited by
the ordinary, untrained individuals in the support groups I
had facilitated. Why was the world so lacking in people who
could just sit gently with us at painful times?

Many of these humble support group participants possessed a practical wisdom of the heart that some highly
educated healers too often lack or gloss over. These experts
could provide amazing remedies, therapies, medicines, and
sound advice, but were not necessarily comforting in their
manner. Sadly, there are even highly lauded spiritual healers
who appear unable or unwilling to offer the sort of warm
greeting and genuine smile that put others at ease.

As a bereavement consultant and educator, I found plenty
of sound, effective resources, courses, and books for understanding grief and loss, for grounding the principles of hospice care, and for facilitating support groups. It surprised
me, however, that very little how-to literature for the aver-
age, nonprofessional layperson was out there about the art

of comforting others in distress. Sure, there were books that showed readers how to comfort *themselves*, such as the Chicken Soup for the Soul books or the Cup of Comfort series, but I could not put my hands on a practical book about how to comfort *others*. It seemed to me that what was sorely needed was a book that explicitly and accessibly spelled out what to say and do to comfort people in distress.

Then, one day, sitting by the Casco Bay, on my favorite mossy spot, gazing in wonder at my beloved blue herons, I had a revelation: I was the one to write the book I couldn't find. I would share with the world what all the wonderful, grieving folks in those support groups as well as professionals in the front lines who possessed the rare gift of comfort had been teaching me for decades—the language of comforting. After all we had been through and witnessed, I knew that we had a book's worth of everyday comforting wisdom to offer. And more than anything, we understood how important it was to make this easy, enjoyable, and practical enough for anyone to read, especially busy, often tired, caregivers.

Welcome, and please join me and the comforting professionals and laypeople who have so graciously offered their wisdom in these pages.

PART ONE

Restoring *a* Lost Art

CHAPTER 1

What Makes People Comforting?

The Language of Comforting

ACCORDING TO the Oxford Dictionary, the word *comfort* originates from the Old French *comfort*, meaning "to be strong with." It's heartening to notice how this definition emphasizes being strong *with*, rather than being strong *for*. Being strong with someone means creating a sanctuary for someone in pain, a respite from the busy, indifferent world around us, just sitting down, listening, and allowing the person to acknowledge his or her pain.

I believe that the reason many of us feel uncomfortable in the role of comforters is because the act of comforting tends to go against our common societal approaches to helping each other. We Americans especially value solution-focused, goal-oriented, and fast, efficient methods for offering assistance to others. We like our efforts to *work*, to "fix it" in a time-measured manner. We think that helping someone in pain means helping them "get over" the problem—and fast.

But with comforting, communication can be slow, uneven, unpredictable, and confusing. As such, we comforters need to "be strong with" the person experiencing distress, accepting with them their uncertainty, a process that requires great patience and calm steadiness.

We are far less comfortable being in a receptive, open, listening role—which is just what people in distress need most. In learning the language of comforting, we might imagine that we are learning the language of a whole different culture, of a foreign land where the customs differ significantly from what we have been socialized to do.

On the following pages are some major contrasts between the messages our mainstream culture tends to believe are helpful and what we in the world of comforting have found to be actually helpful.

✺§ Finding Solutions

MAINSTREAM CULTURE	TO BE COMFORTING
We like to "fix it," get things working again.	We don't offer solutions, but do offer our presence.
We like to advise, to offer answers and remedies.	We listen closely.
We like to take a problem-solving approach.	We wait, let the person find his own words.

❧ Getting Quick Results

MAINSTREAM CULTURE	TO BE COMFORTING
We like to be quick and efficient.	We offer our time, take our time, even just a few minutes. We don't rush.
We are always on the go, on the clock. We like to "get over" things quickly.	We allow someone's grief or trauma to take its own course, have its own pace.
We believe healing means to completely "get over" our losses.	Healing means learning to live with loss, rather than getting over it completely.

❧ Organizing

MAINSTREAM CULTURE	TO BE COMFORTING
We like to know what is going to happen next. We like agendas and to-do lists.	We step into the present moment. We let go of expectations.
We like to have instructions explicated for us.	We accept that comforting can be an unpredictable, disorganized process.
We hate not knowing what to do or say. We avoid silence.	We stay open and let the distressed person talk, even if he or she is upset.

❧ Multitasking

MAINSTREAM CULTURE	TO BE COMFORTING
We do as much as we can, working with interruptions.	We give our undivided attention, with nothing in our hands and no distractions in the room.
We like to click on menus, answer cell phones, pagers, IMs, iPods, faxes, have the TV on.	We communicate in a private, quiet, confidential setting.

🍩 Avoiding Negative Emotions

MAINSTREAM CULTURE	TO BE COMFORTING
We like to cheer people up when they are down.	We don't try to take their pain away. We allow them to feel what they feel.
We like people to be strong and "hold up" under pressure.	We respect a person's right to be vulnerable. We can be a sanctuary, a safe person to be with, when someone falls apart.
We like to use platitudes and teachings from our favorite books, religions, and mentors. We offer popular sayings like "You'll be stronger for this" or "This too shall pass."	Platitudes feel impersonal and preachy.

🍩 Being Productive

MAINSTREAM CULTURE	TO BE COMFORTING
We like to feel useful and helpful.	We accept we may never know if we helped or how we helped.
We like to reassure the ones we are helping that we understand them.	We admit we do not fully understand their journey, but offer to learn more about it with them.

In the Presence of a Comforting Person

Take a moment and remember your response to being with a comforting person. What was it about their presence that heartened you, made you feel lighter? It might have just been a reassuring smile, or a hug. It might have been some

kind words, or a generous act that went beyond the "call
of duty." It might even have been someone simply stopping
to help when we needed directions. One of the best ways
to understand how to be truly comforting is to review our
own encounters with comforting people and notice how they
comforted us.

For many years, in support groups I've facilitated or par-
ticipated in, I have heard the same words used to describe
what it feels like to be effectively comforted. Following are
the most common responses.

UNIVERSAL RESPONSES TO
BEING WITH COMFORTING PEOPLE
❧ *Relief* ❧
"I felt more normal."
"I felt lighter, less burdened."

One woman in a support group for breast cancer survivors, struggling with the double whammy of keeping up her
chemo treatments and facing the foreclosure of her home,
told us how she was comforted by a complete stranger.

> "She was an accounting clerk at the hospital, and I was
> crying hysterically over a bill I couldn't pay, sitting at her
> cubicle. She listened like she really cared for a few minutes,
> and handed me a tissue. I said I couldn't even concentrate
> on reading the forms I had to sign. Then she smiled and

told me that was why she kept a box of tissues at this table, which made me laugh. She added that I was handling my situation as well as anyone she'd known. It was as if she was saying, 'Welcome to the club.' Believe it or not, I settled down quickly after that and managed to fill out the form. The feeling I got from this wonderful person was a sense of being normal, accepted—and this gave me some relief. I felt lighter, less burdened."

❧ *"Heard," Validated* ❧
"My worries and feelings mattered."
"Someone cared enough to listen."

Anne, another member of a support group for chronic illness, told us how life-changing and life-*saving* it was for her to be heard and validated by her doctor.

"Things couldn't have been more depressing. Everyone I knew had tried to talk me out of how bad I was feeling, though I knew I was more exhausted than I'd ever been. People told me I had to buck up and push ahead so I could stay on top of paying the bills. But then, when I saw my doctor, I started telling him more about my symptoms. He cared enough to listen. My worries and feelings mattered. Thankfully, he did some follow-up lab work, because it turned out I had diabetes."

❧ Connected ❧
"I didn't feel alone anymore."
"I belonged there in that room with everyone."

In a support group for people who suffer from anxiety and panic disorder, Jim shared this story about facing his fear of public speaking, and how his sense of connection with his colleagues helped him get through the stage fright.

> "I was freaking out, because I had to give a speech at our annual meeting. I'm petrified of public speaking, and thought I was going to faint! Before my talk, another speaker, one of my colleagues, turned toward me and introduced me. I hadn't expected that. He said kind things about me to the audience, with kudos for my dedication and team spirit. That got me out of my shell, an icebreaker before my speech. I felt I belonged there in that room with everyone, as they smiled warmly at me. I felt safe with them, and realized this speech wasn't the end of the world. Then I gave a pretty good talk after all!"

❧ Calmer ❧
"I realized this speech wasn't the end of the world."
"I felt safe with them."

The kind act of the colleague above who introduced Jim before his speech also made a difference in calming him.

❧ *Loved, Cared for, Appreciated* ❧
"I was touched by his thoughtfulness."
"I felt softer."
"I felt so special to him."

After her sister's death, a woman in a grief support group warmly recounted a touching story about a thoughtful gift made for her by her nephew.

"My nephew, Bob, did a dear and wonderful thing for me when I was getting through my first months after Karen's death. He made me a CD of my favorite songs from the musicals I love. I was so touched by his thoughtfulness. I felt softer, so special to him. It seemed he knew what was in my soul, just by the particular songs he chose."

❧ *Respected, Valued* ❧
"I felt worthy of their time."
"The way they treated me gave me back my dignity."

It's amazing what showing respect for someone's time and effort will do. Dan had been in a support group for job seekers, and spoke about how employers at his interviews had affected his self-esteem.

"I'd been to twelve interviews in the past month, and was getting nowhere fast. To be honest, I didn't feel good about any of those jobs, because no employers were giving me the time of day, let alone decent interviews. They rushed me, seemed distracted, and talked to me like what you hear on robocalls. It was dehumanizing, and I was losing my self-esteem. Finally, I had an interview with a very professional panel of people, and though I was a little nervous, they gave me plenty of time to answer their questions. They were polite and patient and asked really intelligent questions, as if they expected their candidates to be knowledgeable. This made me feel worthy of their time, and encouraged me to be more confident about my qualifications. Also, whether or not I got the job, just the way they treated me gave me back my dignity. It turns out, however, I *did* get that job, and I still feel valued there."

🦋 *Clearer* 🦋
"I could see the next step to take."
"I wasn't so confused."

This woman in a caregiver support group admitted how lost she felt when she first heard of her mother's diagnosis. But with one twenty-minute phone call on a hotline with a well-trained volunteer, things began to get clear.

"I didn't have a clue what to do when I first heard my mother had Alzheimer's. I called a hotline at the Alzheimer's Society, and the worker listened closely to my questions. She normalized some of my feelings of guilt for not doing more sooner. Just sharing with her some of my mixed feelings reassured me that I wasn't so confused after all. Later in the phone call, the worker was able to reflect back to me what my concerns were, showing me she had really followed me, instead of telling me what to do. This helped to clarify my feelings, as well as to make some priorities about how to take care of myself. I could see the next step to take—to go to a caregiver support group."

❦ *Energized* ❧
"I got a shot in the arm."
"This snapped me out of my funk."
"I felt ready to take action."

When Ron's wife lost her job, the same month his daughter had gone to the ER after a car accident, huge financial problems and debt pushed him into foreclosure of his home. He felt terrible as a failed provider for his family, and struggled to keep his own job.

"Losing my home made me feel like a real loser. I was living a nightmare, making it hard to focus on my job. Then, out of the blue, one of my coworkers approached me, and kindly said he was sorry to hear what happened. He invited me to join him for lunch at a diner near our office. He confided to me his brother had also just lost his home, and was feeling pretty bad. He thought maybe I could meet his brother and talk, to support each other, and maybe network together. This gave me a shot in the arm, and snapped me out of my funk. I had been wallowing in feelings of shame, but I felt reassured by my coworker that other people were in the same boat, and that there was no reason to be so hard on myself. Soon I met his brother, John, and we started helping each other look for places to rent. By both of us working on our searches together, I knew that somehow I would get through this time. And week by week, when we checked in with each other on Twitter, I thought that if John could keep going, then I could, too."

❧ *Hopeful, Reassured, Inspired* ❧
"I knew that somehow I would get through this."
"If John could keep on going, then I could, too."

In the story above, hope is restored by the reassuring actions Ron and John have taken together to look for homes.

OUR RESPONSES such as feeling heard, connected, cared for, or hopeful revealed that our comforters were often good listeners, fully present, able to make us feel we were more important than anything else in that moment. Comforting people were usually acting from their empathy. They felt our emotions with us. They were willing to avail their human-to-human, warmhearted qualities to us.

We Are All Comforting in Our Own Ways

Though we know how it feels to be in the presence of a comforting person, we often doubt or undervalue our own innate ability to comfort others. We tend to compare ourselves to images and stereotypes of comforters in our culture. Unfortunately, many of us have gotten the message that only certain people can be truly comforting. We believe some people just have a knack for it, were born with it. We think one has to be exceptionally compassionate, charismatic, or generous, or have years of training in counseling, social work, or pastoral care to be qualified to comfort others. We think we should only comfort people who are going through things familiar to us, and not dare to help when we have little or no experience with their situation. Or we tell ourselves we don't have enough available time on our hands for comforting, that we should leave it to our grandparents or other elders who are freer to give of their time.

These myths about being qualified for comforting have perpetuated stereotypes about comforters, upstaging our natural abilities and common sense. Sadly, we've come to believe we either need to be experts at comforting, or we need to be extraordinarily gifted at it. These idealized, self-imposed expectations can diminish our confidence in our own natural ways of caring for others, and can inhibit us when we are sitting with someone in distress.

Following are common myths about comforters that interfere with trusting our innate abilities to comfort others.

COMMON MYTHS ABOUT COMFORTERS

MYTH: *Comforters are always warm and*
fuzzy, touchy-feely, and big huggers.

Comforting people can be shy, stoic, or reserved, and might prefer to help people in some not-so-touchy ways. The one who runs the errands is as comforting as the one who gives the hugs.

MYTH: *Comforters are only the ones with*
whom we have heart-to-heart talks.

We can comfort others in hundreds of ways: buying their groceries, sending a thoughtful card, playing golf, going out together to a movie, knitting a scarf, walking their dogs. Comforting doesn't always involve conversation.

MYTH: *Comforters always know what to say.*

We don't have to know the right thing to say. Sometimes there is really nothing that can be said. But comforters still offer to show up, even if we don't know what to say, because there are many, many ways to connect and communicate, depending on what that person desires—listening to their favorite songs, bringing catnip for their cat, baking a meat loaf, dumping their trash, playing a game of cards, doing their nails, watching *American Idol* together. We offer our time and our presence, and see what happens. Even Tweeting our comfort in little ways helps, by saying, "I'm thinking about you now, and I hope you are getting through today."

MYTH: *Comforters are always there when*
people need them. ("Call me if you need me.")

We need to be honest about our availability to help, and communicate this clearly. It's always better to be proactive in letting them know what we can actually do for them. We can offer a simple, concrete thing ("I can call you Monday night"). People in distress suffer more when they are "left in the dark" about when contact will be made. No one wants to appear needy by having to call out for help.

MYTH: *Comforters have lots of time to provide enough comfort.*

We can be comforting in a matter of minutes, even in seconds. Little acts of caring can make a big difference for someone in distress.

MYTH: *Comforters are supposed to cheer people up*
when they are down, and tell them to be positive.

Being comforting doesn't mean showering the person in pain with "look at the bright side" platitudes. It is important to acknowledge that the person is in pain as opposed to attempting to get them to "snap out of it."

MYTH: *Comforters need to have much in common*
with the person in distress to be effective.

We can feel someone else's pain even if we cannot identify with their story or background. We are all connected in common sorrows and human life passages. No one has the last word on human suffering.

Complicating these myths about comforters are the market-driven habits of our culture that diminish how much value we place on our innate comforting skills, especially empathic listening. We have learned to speak in dehumanized, commoditized languages, serving our functions to meet bottom lines and deadlines, and to make headlines. In these sink-or-swim environments, comforting people often suppress their wonderful, softhearted tendencies, or avoid high-profile appearances where they would have to go against the ways of their true empathic natures.

I do believe our communication practices, sped up considerably since the advent of the Internet in the mid-'90s, discourage us from slowing down enough to be comforting. This is a hard world to be soft in, to be patient in, to allow vulnerable people to express themselves, to give them the time to find their words. Grieving and devastated people have difficulty concentrating, and struggle for clarity as they battle overwhelming, often mixed and contradictory emotions. They often repeat themselves, or can't get to the point, or are too afraid or depressed to say much. And even though people in distress have great access on the Web to connections with others, they still need our face-to-face, heart-to-heart, hand-to-hand presence. It's ironic how the easier it is to communicate instantly, by cell, by e-mail, by fax, by Twitter, the harder it gets to be fully present with the ones who need us, right where we are.

Given the "nice guys finish last" habits of our culture, it's amazing we have held on to our civility as much as we have, let alone our comforting skills. It's heartening to remember that in spite of how ugly it gets out there, our natural relational ability to provide comfort for others still remains, even if we can't see it ourselves. The fact is that our best comforting qualities often seem so ordinary that we tend to take them for granted. We overlook some of our solid, reliable attributes that may indeed be dearly comforting to others.

Here is a list of comforting traits I have gathered from responses of more than five hundred participants in recent years, from teaching classes in the art of comforting, training group facilitators, and facilitating support groups. I promise that you will find that you possess a number of the following twenty qualities, and I invite you to use them as your foundation for building upon your comforting skills.

The Top Twenty Attributes of Comforting People

BEING PRESENT AND LISTENING

Of all the qualities of comforting, the most essential are our presence and good listening, laying the foundation for all other comforting skills.

Our best human strengths and virtues will not be effective without the basic, underlying ability to be present to each other. We can have great intentions, be spiritually motivated, be politically correct, be organized and smart, or be downright nice, but if we don't bring ourselves fully into the present moment with others, we lose our attunement to one another's needs, feelings, and cues.

"Being there" for someone does not necessarily mean being *always* there, but it does require us to be *all* there, with our undivided attention. Being present involves engaging our nonverbal communication, our facial expressions, eye contact, gestures, and voice intonations, as the language of comforting is at least 80 percent nonverbal. (Though some people say they listen better when they are doodling or texting, it is not comforting for the person in distress speaking to us, who needs to see our responses.)

PRESENT—*"there," listens well, gives their full
attention, in the moment, focused*

In the language of comforting, listening is as important as using words. In the *Oxford Dictionary*, to *listen* means to "pay attention to." If all we did was listen, paying full attention, we would be well on our way to being comforting.

When we pay full attention to someone, we are showing this person that he or she matters to us, that their dilemma matters to us. When it comes to comforting, the simplest, most honest human-to-human kinds of communication serve us best. Sometimes all we can say is we are sorry things are so hard, and be with someone in naked silence.

Here is a story about the power of our presence from Patricia Ellen, a grief counselor and chaplain, working with grieving families at the Center for Grieving Children in

Portland, Maine. (She will be profiled later as one of our guides to the practice of comforting.)

Patricia's Story of Being Comforted

1988 was a time of excruciating grief and darkness after my son, Doug, fourteen years old, had committed suicide. Eight months after his death, I was comforted by a particular experience that happened very gently and naturally one summer evening in Portsmouth, New Hampshire.

Two friends came to visit me and invited me to take a long walk with them. We walked mostly in silence by lush gardens and trees in the balmy summer air. My friends only said about four sentences for the whole evening. But in that silence I felt their love and care in waves of comfort streaming from their hearts. In their soft presence, I softened along with them and opened up to behold the beauty of nature around me.

It was a transformative experience for me to feel the comfort of my dear friends and the earth, mostly without words, teaching me the sacredness of being present.

Silence can truly be golden if we take the leap of faith that listening is all we need to do. Moments of silence are sacred, bonding us in soulful ways, sometimes the best medicine of all.

The Importance of Empathy

NEXT TO BEING PRESENT AND LISTENING WELL,
THE SECOND MOST IMPORTANT COMFORTING
TRAIT IS EMPATHY.

EMPATHIC—*senses the feelings of another person*

Empathy is feeling what another human being feels, whether or not we identify with their beliefs, status, or background. We can feel the sorrow of someone else, even if their life experience is nothing like ours, because we all know sorrow by having lived through loss in our own lives. Our commonality of human challenges and suffering is far greater than our separate ideologies, religions, cultures, or genders.

Most of us possess a great amount of empathy, but, unfortunately, our culture has developed uncomforting habits that suppress this vital capacity. One destructive habit in particular is the tendency to compare one person's suffering to another's. And this can be disastrous for our language of comforting.

In our society, we often find ourselves getting sucked into downward spirals of "their-misery-is-worse-than-yours" comparisons and contrasts, mistakenly thinking we are lessening someone's distress by "putting it in perspective": "You think your foreclosure was bad—but look, the Hurricane Katrina folks had it much worse than you." (Or the homeless folks in tent cities have it worse, or the poor kids in the ghettos of New York, or in the refugee settlements in

Darfur, or in the slums of Brazil or India. . . .) But it's just not comforting for anyone in distress to be compared to anyone else, anywhere else.

Though in our legal and financial systems, we compare and quantify pain and suffering constantly, this practice does not apply to our role as comforters with one another. If we are to be effective comforters, it is better to respect that pain is downright painful for anyone and everyone, *whatever* the reason or cause.

A woman in a divorce support group, Jan, tells us her story about two married women friends who did not open their hearts with empathy, but instead compared her situation to theirs, trying to downplay her distress.

Meeting together at a Thai restaurant, Jan told her friends how hard it was adjusting to life as a single woman. Her friends began comparing their marital woes to her woes, chiding her, "It's lonelier being in a bad marriage than being single. You're free now. You have a whole new life ahead of you." Her friends might have meant well, trying to convince Jan she shouldn't be feeling so bad, but this actually minimized her pain. Jan got the not-so-comforting message that her distressed feelings were unwarranted, according to her friends, and therefore she was not worthy of their empathy. She felt worse, even lonelier, after hearing their comments.

Jan lingered at the restaurant after the two women left, and the Thai restaurant owner, a woman about her age, chatted with her for a while, as business was slow that night. She told Jan her story of coming to America, and how she had left behind much of her family. She was struggling and working hard to raise her two children without her husband, who had recently been forced to return to Thailand.

Touched, Jan briefly shared she was on her own, too. "It's hard, isn't it? My marriage ended and I'm trying to find my way."

The Thai woman asked, "Do you have kids?"

When Jan answered she did not have children, the woman softly touched her arm and said, "So, you are all alone, no husband, no kids . . . that sounds sad. I am so sorry to hear this."

Fighting back her tears, Jan smiled and thanked her. This woman had no idea how much her simple words meant to her. They genuinely felt one another's sorrow.

When we don't compare suffering between ourselves, we can indeed comfort one another with our empathy, whether it be with toddlers with scraped knees, with lovesick adolescents, with heartbroken widows, or with hungry refugees.

No matter what society tells us about how different we are, we all have the same feelings at heart. Certainly our beloved animal companions know what we feel, as do our children and our greatest artists, storytellers, and healers, but many of us have suppressed this beautiful gift of empathy.

GENUINE—*sincere, has integrity*

The Thai woman in the previous story about empathy was willing to open up and show her genuine feelings and her true self. It was comforting just to see the honest caring in her eyes. When we really mean what we say, sometimes we don't have to say as much.

RESPECTFUL—*honors people as human beings first and foremost above all roles or status*

If we think back and remember times people have comforted us, we can review how they gave us their respect, or at least their respectful courtesy. They did not push us, rush us, dismiss us, stereotype us, manipulate us. They listened, and welcomed our opinion, even if they did not agree with it. They saw the dignity in us, and honored us.

Comforters deeply value all the years we have spent dealing with the universal challenges of being human, whether we were getting to age forty, or thirteen, or eighty. They believe everyone works hard to get to where they are, so we are all important.

The comforting people we know are often quite gifted at making people feel vital to any meeting, gathering, or group. Good group facilitators, for example, encourage everyone's opinions, but also respect those who do not feel ready or willing to speak.

PATIENT—*allows people to move, speak, and think at their own pace; doesn't rush people*

It's a great relief for people in distress to find a patient person. Often people in times of loss and crisis have difficulty trying to explain their needs or their desires, and others tune them out before they can finish what they are saying. Unfortunately in our culture, some people rush them to "get to the point," or push them, saying, "Stop repeating yourself—you've already said that twice!" People in pain or in crisis cannot concentrate well, and need our help by allowing them to gather their thoughts, or maybe to think out loud until they are clear with their message.

CARING—*kind, compassionate, thoughtful, considerate*
In the language of comforting, the little acts of caring mean everything. One recently bereaved, elderly man told me how comforting it was to have his shy, fifteen-year-old neighbor come by every day to help him walk his dogs. "We hardly ever said a word, but that boy loved my dogs and showed up right at four o'clock every afternoon, for about thirty minutes, rain or shine. He played Frisbee with my dogs and perked them up—and that perked me up, too."

RELIABLE—*dependable, trustworthy, will do what*
they say they will do, keeps commitments
Reliability is extremely important for people in distress. In their complicated, uncertain, and overwhelming situations, they need to count on us. It's better to offer a single commitment we can honor realistically, a sure bet, rather than make a promise that might overextend us. It's safer to stand by one simple, specific act such as making a phone call on Monday night, instead of promising to call every week, or assuring them, "I'm there for you—just call anytime." We honestly

need to assess and clarify our availability and capacity to be in the comforting role for someone, no matter how much we care. We can only "be there" when we offer the specifics and follow through.

I've heard grieving and distraught people lament how others didn't follow through with their promises, which hurt them more than anyone's lack of affection or warmth. Their friendly, sunny friends who promised to "be there" for them "fell off the face of the earth" after they dropped off their casseroles during the first days of the tragedy. Surprisingly, sometimes the more modest, "sensible" people in the background turned out to be the real comforters, checking in regularly for many weeks afterward. These true-blue folks brought by vegetables from their garden, or met us for coffee after church, or picked up our mail while we were stuck in the hospital.

CLEAR—*lets people in distress know what we can
realistically do for them, and clarifies our role as comforters,
while keeping firm with our boundaries*

Comforters cannot be everything to everybody. We need to make it clear the ways we can and cannot comfort others. This is an important aspect of being reliable and realistically available to people in distress. Our boundaries keep us from getting hooked into doing more than we are comfortable doing, and prevent us from feelings of resentment from doing too much.

One newly bereaved man in a grief support group tells us how a little clarity goes a long way in comforting:

"It's funny how the person who was most comforting to me was only able to see me once a month. Though plenty of people said they would stop in and see me more often, half the time they didn't, and I wished they had not been so vague—leaving me hanging. But my friend was very clear and direct about what he could actually do. He even admitted he didn't know how to talk about my grief issues, but he did say he could at least be my movie buddy. One Saturday every month, we went to see a movie and then shared a pizza. Perfect."

WARM—*welcoming, gracious, greets others with a sincere smile, approachable*

Being able to greet and introduce one another is key to establishing a comforting encounter. The art of graciousness is a more public aspect of comforting that we sometimes see in our media.

If we think of our favorite talk show hosts and news anchors, those who have been going strong for many years, we can observe their remarkable greeting and hosting skills. They use their warmth and graciousness in quite varied ways to get their guests to feel comfortable at the start of their interviews. If we have a favorite talk show host, news anchor, or journalist, we might study what it is that makes them comforting in how they handle their guests. I've heard people in support groups comment on their favorites:

"Ellen DeGeneres seems relaxed and easygoing. Her dancing thing always cracks me up—a great icebreaker."

"Ann Curry's warm voice is calming, and her eye contact with her guests is welcoming."

"Bill Moyers listens so quietly, patiently, and has a soft voice."

ACCEPTING—*open-minded, nonjudgmental,*
receptive, willing to learn from others

We all know people who sincerely seem to be interested in other people, curious about them, yet tolerant when opinions clash. They like learning from others, asking questions and exploring different perspectives, whether or not they fit with their own worldview.

Here is what a cancer support group member said about an open-minded, friendly hairstylist she sees every other month:

"Betty doesn't miss a thing. She remembers everything I told her two months ago, and asks how Jamie's doing every time I see her. It is downright comforting to have someone who wants to hear what's going on, following my family's ups and downs. She doesn't judge me. She just seems fascinated in what I tell her. I confide things with her about Jamie I'd never tell to my closer friends."

CALM—*centered, steady, quiet, still, serene*

Some comforters emanate calmness and groundedness. They don't get rattled too easily, so there is no need to censor what we say, pile on the Teflon, or walk on eggshells.

A colleague of mine, a hospice nurse, possesses a lovely steadiness and calmness, enhancing the tranquil, quiet environment of the hospice house and gardens. Families seek her out when they feel frantic, and she makes a difference in their lives within a few minutes in her presence. Her nonverbal communication is calming, with her tone of voice, gestures, and facial expressions.

HOPEFUL—*believes that people will find their own*
way to healing, instills hope without being
"preachy" or giving advice

Though it may seem obvious, it's comforting to declare that comforters of our world tend to have a hopeful outlook on humanity. They believe in the resourcefulness of our human hearts and spirits. Often highly comforting people have suffered their own grueling slew of ordeals, even inhumane ordeals, and have come through it all to love their lives as well as the true grit in all of us.

Jeff Lewis, a nurse practitioner working at a veterans hospital (one of our comforters profiled later), tells us he encourages hope in his patients, even at the end of their lives. He helps them find what keeps them hopeful—what keeps them going. One of Jeff's patients told him, though facing only a few weeks of life in his terminal condition, "I'm holding on so I can hug my grandson when he comes back from Iraq next month."

HUMBLE—*honors his or her own human limitations and vulnerabilities*

Often we seek out comforters who stand modestly in the background. They quietly offer their comfort without expectations or need for acknowledgment. They've observed the humbling truth that no one human being has the last word on any subject, and accepts their limitations in seeing all of "the big picture."

Having humility helps us understand the shadow sides and vulnerabilities of ourselves and others. A good comforter has faced the good, the bad, and the ugly in themselves, and has been able to honestly integrate these aspects into their love of humanity. These are the people we know who have "been there," who can handle hearing about our most vulnerable, shameful, or embarrassing moments.

SUPPORTIVE, VALIDATING—*offers words, gestures, and actions that build on a person's strengths and preferences, "strengths-based"*

Some people are brilliant at reflecting back to us our best qualities. They "get" us, maybe better than we "get" ourselves. Good comforters often have this ability to hone in on our strengths, shine a light on them, and bring them forth. They show us how to build on these qualities in ourselves without preaching to us about "living up to our potential" or giving us pep talks. Instead, they just believe in us, period.

One of the best career counselors I ever met was a genius at validating the strengths of her clients. She helped clients write amazing résumés that perfectly described their best qualities. When these clients went on job interviews, they glowed from their faith in the gifts of their character and accomplishments. They had been validated, with the "good to go" stamp of this counselor, and impressed employers with their confidence.

APPRECIATIVE—*grateful, recognizes the value of others, and "counts" their blessings*

There's nothing like a heartfelt thank-you from someone. Showing our appreciation for others provides relief from the hard tasks and chores of our daily life. Taking a moment to express gratitude is a marvelous comforting tool for any occasion or group. It creates a bit of breathing space to pause and give thanks, as well as makes a safe place for counting our blessings that have appeared along the way.

GENEROUS—*giving, without expectations, often spontaneously*

Some people surprise us with spontaneous acts of generosity. Here's one example from a man in a chemical dependency rehab program, who believes this encounter opened his eyes to his recovery.

"I met an old friend for coffee. At first, I thought we'd just be together for about an hour, but afterward, he offered to walk with me to a bookstore I loved. He said he was enjoying my company, and wanted to spend time browsing through books we both liked. We had a good time, and we bought a couple of great inspirational memoirs. Sometimes the unexpected things people do with us are the most fun and rewarding."

GENTLE, TENDER—*soft, can sensitively allow for the other person to respond*

The gentlest gestures, such as handing someone a tissue, or softly touching their arm can make a world of difference in trying times. Here is what a nervous flyer told us:

"I hate being on airplanes, especially in turbulence. It was pretty bumpy, and I was not doing well. A sweet older woman sitting next to me gently touched my arm, and asked if I was okay. I must have looked really pale and awful. I reached to hold her hand, and looking at her sparkling eyes and soft smile, I could see she was really sensitive and understanding about this."

ADAPTABLE—*can respond to changes, flexible, resourceful, can "go with the flow"*

Comforting people are often good at thinking on their feet and going with the flow of the moment. Without being over-accommodating, they can adjust schedules, topics, or settings to help other people feel more comfortable. Even just tweaking a few words or details for a meeting or a speech can put people at ease. They stay attuned to the mood, needs, and nonverbal messages of those around them, and sense when to make adjustments to enhance communication.

WISE/EXPERIENCED—*mature, has life experience, has been through demanding challenges and losses*

Sometimes a wiser individual sits in the background, quietly listening to an awkward or painful conversation about a difficult issue, and then, at a well-timed interval, offers a personal story to shed light on a particular concern. Our elders often have emotional maturity and a seasoned perspective on our life's challenges. Comforting people have usually gone through their own losses and have gained some insight on their own rocky journeys. Without giving advice or interfering in what we choose to do, they share their own stories of what they've learned.

STRONG—*persevering, resilient, enduring, confident*

Especially when we are ill or feeling tired and weak, it is comforting to have someone around who is energetic, strong, and confident. These hardy folks can give us a boost, helping us to do the physically demanding or emotionally draining things, such as dumping the trash, cleaning the cat litter box, or calling the insurance company to straighten out claims forms and bills. They are up to the task when we feel incapable of handling it.

. . .

FORTUNATELY, WE ALL HAVE SOME of these comforting traits. Our unique clusters of attributes define the ways we are most authentic in comforting others, though some traits may strengthen or diminish over the years, reflecting our values and goals. Most people find they have certain highly reliable attributes, and put these into practice as relational skills throughout their lifetime.

Looking over this list again, we might assess our own comforting traits, choosing our top five strengths that stand out. Or, if we want to use a bit more scrutiny (in a comforting way, of course), we could score ourselves, ranging from 1 (lowest) to 10 (highest) on our various comforting abilities.

Being present and listening

Empathic

Respectful

Patient

Caring and compassionate

Genuine

Reliable

Clear

Warm and gracious

Accepting

Calm

Hopeful

Humble

Supportive and validating

Appreciative

Generous

Gentle

Adaptable

Wise

Strong

For example, picking five of these attributes that best reflect me, I am strong in the qualities of empathy, warmth, supportiveness, reliability, and genuineness. My most prominent and enduring trait is empathy.

My lowest five, my least developed qualities, include being present, calm, patient, and accepting. I am still not a very good listener (I give myself a score of 4), even though I've had gazillions of hours of training in counseling practices! My empathy gets me too carried away with another person's emotions, and it all goes to my mouth. I need to be careful that I don't blurt things out, working at taking breaths, focusing my attention, and doing little tension relievers to stay centered. Playing to my strengths, I tend to be a better comforter with groups, as a speaker and trainer, rather than in one-on-one work, though I am eternally improving. Certainly, with my "lovingly honest" colleagues and loved ones, I practice my not-so-developed comforting skills, especially good listening.

Our best comforting traits are there for us to claim and

nurture, foundations for building our skills and practices as comforters, for others as well as ourselves. Introverts among us can be comforting with their quiet presence and calm, patient listening. Talkative types can share their caring and warmth by advocating for their loved ones. Accepting, humble, and nonjudgmental people can sit down with us when we feel too ashamed or embarrassed to go to a support group. Reliable, kindhearted, but not-so-touchy-feely types can comfort us with little acts of caring such as making a meal, running an errand, or doing a special favor. Certainly, any thoughtful act of kindness can be comforting to anyone. We don't need any extraordinary comforting qualifications to comfort people when we genuinely care and take action.

CHAPTER 2

Comforting in Action

A Calling

FIVE YEARS AGO, I faced something worse than compassion fatigue—a sense of dismay at the lack of compassion throughout our society. What was happening to our safety nets for people in need? Like many Americans, I was aghast at the cuts in social services around the country amid rising health care, education, housing, and child care costs. The once-flourishing mental health and vocational rehabilitation agencies where I had worked back in the 1990s were now cutting vital programs for poor and isolated people coping with serious mental illness. And more cuts were on the way. I watched some of my rehabilitation colleagues growing more despondent and cynical. It was getting tougher and tougher out there for those of us who were frail, fragile, or poor, without social support systems in their lives.

Like many of my former clients who had been "dumped" by their social services providers, I felt undervalued and dehumanized by my own health care providers. I didn't feel

I mattered or had a voice when I was reaching out to the people I needed to help me. Trying to find someone to really hear me and give me the time of day had nearly become a full-time job. Going from doctor to doctor, I had been seeking help for some strange, troubling sensations in my heart and upper abdomen, but no one had listened carefully and patiently enough, and my symptoms had been dismissed as anxiety. I had expected to be taken seriously when I tried to describe a frightening incident of nearly collapsing in a bookstore. Instead, I was told to take relaxation classes and do more walking.

To make a long, frustrating story short, I finally located two astute and respectful female physicians who ordered a thorough workup, including an echocardiogram, stress test, many EKGs, and other lab tests. They found problems in the functioning of my left ventricle, and needed to control my blood pressure and heart rhythms more aggressively with several stronger medications. If I hadn't listened to my intuition and my own heart, and if no one had listened to me, I may have ended up with heart failure within a few years.

My physician, a D.O., and later my cardiologist, were two women who skillfully practiced the language of comforting. Fully present, listening with respect and empathy, they gently provided me with a vital opportunity to speak up honestly, thoroughly, and comfortably. Not only was I heard, supported, and calmed in their presence, I was literally given the right treatment, medically, ethically, and compassionately. Finally, I felt human again. Normal again. Dignified again. My heart disease was not "all in my head" after all.

Profoundly inspired by the life-saving implications of my providers' comforting practices, I had a revelation: Comforting skills were more than soft, feel-good accessories for enhancing our connections—they were essential for clear, open, and honest communication. If people didn't feel genuinely welcomed and encouraged to tell what really had happened to them, then what did our providers and loved ones have to go on? The art of comforting meant creating a safe place for telling the truth, which, as in my case, could even save a life. We needed the "soft" skills of comforting to establish reliable lines of communication, especially in places where "hard" medical science was supposed to heal us.

After reflecting on the importance of the comforting skills my two doctors had practiced so well, I felt called to learn more about this practical wisdom from other professionals. I wanted to find compassionate comforters skilled at creating safe places for communicating difficult and painful things, for telling the truth of our experiences, without being rushed, judged, pegged, or ignored. These comforters were out there, busy on their jobs, but gifted at giving us their genuine acceptance, respect, and care when we were feeling vulnerable. They could assure us that, in a world hard to be soft in, we could be little sanctuaries of comfort for each other.

Calling All Comforters!

I didn't need to search the planet for highly comforting people to interview. I already knew many remarkable professionals who had heartened and motivated me over the years, when my compassion had needed a boost. I started rounding up exceptionally comforting colleagues in different occupations from several states I had lived in and visited. I was also given recommendations of other comforters by my colleagues.

Gradually and naturally, through casual discussions, and later, through more formal interviews, I gathered the insights and suggestions of thirteen comforters. They each had their own unique perspectives, viewed from their particular occupation, but, reassuringly, I discovered they were all speaking the same language of comforting, putting universal comforting skills into practice every day in their jobs. They might be rushing through their days as a nurse practitioner, a grief counselor, or a police liaison, but they each had effective and quick ways of putting comforting into action. As I learned their how-to's of comforting, I was relieved to discover many of their practices only involved a minute of their time, though making a huge difference in the people they served. To my surprise and joy, I found their recommended activities to be highly applicable for most of us, at home and at work.

Every one of my highly comforting guides told me their

most recommended practice was to establish a human-to-human connection *before* "getting down to business." Putting the human relationship first, no matter how much we had to accomplish, was at the heart of comforting. Above and beyond our agendas, our titles, our purpose, our roles, honoring the relationship for its own sake was essential for comforting in all personal and professional activities.

Comforters were skilled at greeting us warmly and inviting us into their space, making us feel we belonged there with them, no matter what the purpose of the occasion was supposed to be. We lost the magic of a comforting moment when we rushed to extract and abstract from someone what we needed to meet our goals and serve our purpose. We dampened our sense of belonging with each other if we bypassed the little acts of caring that didn't quite fit our schedules.

Expediency was the greatest threat to comforting, according to my colleagues. If people were only there to serve a purpose, to move along in our assembly-line mentality of being productive, then, of course, our souls got the not-so-comforting message that we only mattered for our functions. And that made us feel like machines, commodities, objects, and not warm-blooded, caring human beings.

It was possible to comfort people even in hectic jobs with demanding schedules, and establishing good connections saved time in the long run. A little bit of rapport-building at the beginning made all the difference. Taking a few minutes to connect with a person individually could ensure good communication at later times when that person's concerns became more complicated and stressful.

Following is a list of the core comforting skills displayed universally by the master comforters I interviewed:

1. Preparation skills for comforters to inform themselves about the situation being faced by the person in distress before meeting with them.
2. Greeting skills for establishing a warm and welcoming connection, and putting the person at ease.
3. Acquainting, orienting, and hosting skills to calm, support, and reassure the person in distress, especially when in unfamiliar surroundings and when meeting new people.
4. Skills in creating comforting environments and atmospheres for working, healing, and recreation.
5. Conversation skills to foster comfortable, relaxed opportunities to communicate with empathic comments and open-ended questions.
6. Facilitation skills for guiding and engaging people in comforting activities such as playing board games, baking bread, or beading necklaces.

In this chapter, five talented, friendly, and articulate professional caregivers, all with at least fifteen years' experience in their fields, will be serving as personal guides to these skills and practices of comforting. They will each show us how they establish human-to-human connections in their busy jobs, as well as their concrete, simple ways of comforting others, verbally and nonverbally.

But just as important as their practical how-to's of comforting, I couldn't help noticing the outstanding personal qualities of these individuals. Each comfort guide possesses distinct attributes, and generously applies them when sharing their knowledge and skills, putting comfort into action in their own way. If we recall the Twenty Top Comforting Qualities introduced earlier, we can see how each guide shines from their own comforting qualities, playing to their strengths. Though all comfort guides have their bundle of abilities, and all possess a good amount of empathy and presence, particular atributes stand out in each of them.

· ❧ ·

PUTTING THE HUMAN CONNECTION ABOVE EVERYTHING ELSE

Jeff Lewis, N.P.

Nurse Practitioner, Cardiology Unit (2002-2008)

Togus Veterans Affairs Medical Center, Augusta, Maine

> *Anytime a patient shares something personal about their history, I tell them, "It's a privilege to know this about you."*

Core Comforting Qualities: Appreciation and Respect

Feeling shy and a little nervous about calling Jeff at work, I was hoping I could just leave a friendly, concise voice mail asking him for an interview. Instead, he answered the phone. I told him who I was and what my call was about in my nine-second, well-rehearsed blurb, and modestly asked, "Do you have a minute?"

To my surprise and relief, he cheerfully replied, "I've got exactly three minutes."

At the end of our three minutes, we had scheduled a series of short interviews during his lunch breaks on Mondays at Togus Veterans Affairs Medical Center. It was now four minutes into our call, and I was aware our time was up. "That was a productive three minutes, and I'll let you go . . . thank you so much."

In closing Jeff said, "Thank *you* for calling, a nice surprise today. It's an honor to be asked to be interviewed about something as important as comforting—and I've got some great stories to share with you."

My instincts that Jeff would be an ideal candidate as a guide to comforting were validated by this brief exchange. He could work wonders in four minutes of a conversation, by putting a person at ease while getting down to business. Yes, there did exist in this world some kind, respectful, and appreciative individuals who could be comforting and productive at the same time, even at crowded, humongous veterans hospitals.

On his Monday lunch breaks on the cardiology unit, Jeff and I have had wonderful heart-to-heart talks about comforting. We were interrupted about every six minutes by patients popping into his office, and each time Jeff would calmly and masterfully switch gears back to focusing on our conversation, tuning out everything around him, listening closely, as if I mattered more than anything in the entire hospital, at least for a few minutes.

Our meetings have convinced me it's possible to be fully present, comfortable, and happily engaged in the most hectic of settings. A few minutes of Jeff's attention is fulfilling and downright fun. Giving me his smiles, nods, sympathetic shrugs, laughs, and "I know what you mean" expressions, he heartily follows what I'm saying about my passion for the art of comforting. With his lively curiosity and rapt interest in my questions, we go through scenarios to describe how he comforts his patients.

"My patients blow me away." He shakes his head in amazement. "They're stronger than you think—they comfort *me* half the time."

Watching the faces of Jeff's patients light up when they enter his office, how he welcomes and attends to them in a brisk and affectionate way, I can see why he is so popular with veterans, and why award plaques cover his wall. And as I learned more about Jeff's remarkable background, I discovered that he's had a lifetime of dedication to comforting people in distress and trauma.

"My father died at only thirty-nine years of age when I was twelve. He had been diagnosed with colon cancer, had a colostomy, and later the cancer spread to his liver. I observed how well he adapted to living with a terminal illness, and learned much about comforting from him.

"Though he was the one with the illness—the one in pain—he gave *us* comfort by showing us how much we meant to him. He strongly believed in keeping positive, not for himself so much as for others around him. He told me repeatedly, 'If you are having a good day, you can make someone's bad day better, but when you are having a bad day, you can make someone's good day worse.' He taught me that we had a great effect on each other's days, for better or worse, just with our demeanor, mood, and outlook. With his short life, he showed me that we mattered by making others feel they mattered.

"Before my dad got cancer, I had been a typical self-centered and manipulative kid, who couldn't have cared less if I had teased some classmate at school or picked a fight with my brother. But once my father was ill, I watched my worried mother and siblings trying to take care of him. They were so afraid they weren't doing enough for him. He reassured them by holding their hands and telling them how well they were helping him. I saw how he comforted the comforters and the comforters comforted him. Soon, encouraged and coached by my father, I was putting into practice some comforting behaviors of my own, and felt the difference in the tension level of our household. To my surprise, I discovered I liked being a comforter, a nurturer, a caregiver. No wonder I ended up working in nursing and emergency medical services!"

In his teens, he volunteered for his local EMS (Emergency Medical Services) department, and learned to calm and attend to frightened patients in ambulances. He later served as a part-time paramedic firefighter for twelve years, while working as an ER nurse for fifteen years. He has been a nurse-practitioner at Togus Veterans Affairs Medical Center for seven years. All of his positions have involved following strict, rapid-response protocols for patients in acute crisis. Almost daily for thirty years, he has practiced the skills of comforting in the most dire, life-and-death situations.

Wherever he goes, he taps the nurturing wisdom of his father. "Every day, when I walk into this hospital to work, I carry with me my father's words and love of life. I practice 'having a good day' for the sake of others around me, and this certainly helps my day, too." If anyone in the world knows how to create a comfort zone in the midst of chaos, Jeff does.

JEFF'S MOST IMPORTANT QUALITIES
OF A COMFORTING PERSON

Jeff designated the following as the most vital abilities of comforters:

- Warm and welcoming, takes time to greet the person

> "Being a comforting presence means paying personal attention to the patient and getting to know them as a real person. It's essential that we take the time to establish rapport and trust first, before we do anything else. I've learned that if I rush through my first few minutes with a

patient, preoccupied with treating them before I really listen to them, then it's harder for both of us to move forward with each other as partners in healing. So, taking the time at the beginning to get to know a patient really saves time in the long run."

- Appreciates what a person has to say, and shows it

  "I deeply believe in the power of appreciating people. Showing my gratitude and respect, especially with veterans, has helped to develop healthy, trusting bonds. My father taught me the benefits of letting people know how important they are, by recognizing the ways they are contributing to the relationship, not just to the 'program.' Expressing gratitude openly to people creates an opportunity to point out their strengths, values, and personal traits, a natural kind of positive reinforcement."

- Can tune out distractions and tune in to the person
- Finds out what is comforting for that person in particular

JEFF'S COMFORTING PRACTICES IN HIS WORK
1. Learn about the person's background and situation before you meet with them—if that information is available.

Jeff believes it's important to prepare ourselves with any accessible information before approaching the person we want to help.

"Before meeting with the person, I find out about the person's situation with any accurate information that is available. This helps me think ahead about some of the issues the person may be dealing with. I study their social support networks, and especially pay attention to people who have little social support. I check to see if they have sustained any major losses recently. For example, when I see that their spouse has died in the past year, or that they have recently relocated to a nursing facility, I am prepared to address any grief or stress that might interfere with their medical treatment."

Jeff says another reason to find out about the person's situation is that we need to avoid asking them too many questions. "The person may be in emotional or physical pain, and not be ready to articulate and explain what has been going on very clearly or specifically."

Extreme stress and grief can affect our cognitive abilities, our memory, our concentration, and our reasoning skills. It's not very comforting for distressed people to answer a barrage of questions from someone on a probing, fact-finding mission. We need to be gentle with our "what happened?" questioning while we interact with the person. We might not get all the information, or the correct information, all at once. But gradually, by accepting and appreciating what they are able to tell us with our patience, good listening, and gratitude, the person might eventually be better able to communicate more information.

2. Welcome people with warm, respectful greetings,
and introduce yourself and your role.

I watched Jeff in action at the hospital, as he welcomed his patients and enjoyed the back and forth banter of their casual conversation. It was obvious the patients relaxed within only thirty seconds of chatting. Jeff says:

> "I introduce myself, telling them that I am a nurse practitioner by choice (why I chose this career over being a cardiologist), and invite them to use me as a 'go-to' person for their questions. Then, I ask them what's been going on in their world, and listen closely to what they tell me has happened recently. Once again, taking the time at the beginning to get to know a person really pays off later in more efficient communication when facing challenges along their course of treatment."

Jeff's words as a nurse-practitioner apply to all of us as comforters. Greetings are essential for establishing a comforting encounter. When we walk into an unfamiliar building to meet a new provider, or we travel to meet a friend at their home, or we meet a new colleague, having our host meet us and greet us with welcoming gestures relaxes and reassures us. We get the message: "It's good to see you!" But, when we don't get that message, we worry about what might be wrong, and maybe even fret that the host does not honestly want to meet us. It's not only rude not to greet people, it's downright destructive to establishing trust and basic eye-to-eye contact.

> *3. Follow the lead of the people you're serving, and*
> *share in their concerns. They give you cues as*
> *to what concerns are bothering them.*

When we comfort someone, we need to begin with the understanding that even if their concern doesn't seem to us to be the "real" issue or the "problem," we need to respect the reality of their pain, and tune in through their eyes to how their situation is impacting them. In Jeff's work, he needs to identify the concerns of his patients because these can be barriers to their treatment. It might be their financial concerns, transportation problems, insurance issues, housing issues, marital issues, or dietary issues that might interfere with the patient focusing on their treatment. Jeff needs to know these and address them, but first he uses his active listening skills to elicit from patients those barriers. "I've seen some patients completely unable to relax without their rosaries, who needed to hold them in their hands the whole time they were being examined. So, I take their personal requests seriously, if this means they are able to feel more comforted and relaxed in a medical setting. Or, say, if someone is really angry, and that presents a barrier, I need to support them in vocalizing what is making them upset. It helps to establish trust by allowing that person to vent their concerns or complaints while I listen and take the time we need."

We comforters need to show our appreciation and respect for any obstacles or problems the person in distress is communicating to us. Comforters are not the ones to judge these barriers as "excuses," "rationalizations," or "BS" when we don't agree that their "issues" are keeping them from taking action or making important decisions. As comforters, we accept that any concerns a person in distress shares with us are whatever that person is ready to handle or address. Maybe later that person will be ready to face challenges in a more head-on way, but in the acute stages of crisis or grief, a person may not be ready for that.

4. *Find what keeps the person hopeful.*

Instilling hope is a powerful comforting tool. Jeff emphasizes, "We can listen closely and discover whatever it is that person is looking forward to—and it just might surprise us." Comforters don't have to offer cheery, hopeful platitudes, or "you'll be fine" assurances, but they can help the person in distress connect with something they hope to do in the near future. It could be a visit with a pet therapy dog, or a Sunday dinner with their sister, or a long-awaited movie release. I've known people who held on to their sanity just by looking forward to the latest episode of *Dancing with the Stars*. Jeff says even people at the end of their lives with terminal illnesses find things to keep them going strong.

"Keeping hope alive is important, even when the person is facing terminal illness. Instilling hope doesn't mean giving people false hope or trying to cheer them up. It means listening to their hopes, joining them in envisioning their dreams, wishes, and goals, whether they have six months to live or sixty years. As a cardiac nurse-practitioner, for the sake of their hearts, I try to keep their spark of hope alive—such as helping someone live for a few more weeks to make it to the birth of their grandchild."

5. *Show your appreciation when people tell you personal things about themselves.*

As comforters, when people in distress offer to tell us confidential and deeply private things, we can gently express our appreciation for this. It takes courage for people to open up and trust each other with painful issues. We might say, as comforters, "I am honored that you shared this with me. It sounds like this was hard to tell anyone." Here's what Jeff says to his patients that confide in him:

"Any time a patient shares something important about themselves, I tell them, 'It is a privilege to know this about you.' I let them know how deeply grateful I am to be the one they have confided in, even though, as a health care professional I am 'supposed' to know their health histories or habits. Histories are personal, and sometimes hard to share. Working with veterans here at Togus, I am always honored, sometimes amazed, when they open up with their honesty and humility. This deepens our relationship, and they will keep coming back to me when they need to ask hard questions about their prognosis or their functional limitations."

How to Give "Bad News" in a Comforting Way

Sometimes, unfortunately, we find ourselves in the position of having to give bad news to our loved ones or others we are serving, and the delicate language of comforting needs to be put into practice. Jeff has much experience with this difficult role of being the messenger with bad news. He encourages us to be honest, humble, and gentle in our approach.

"We can beat ourselves up worrying about how to tell people bad news. We try to anticipate how they will respond and imagine all kinds of ways to say things right. When I've second-guessed what people were going to say, I've usually been wrong. I've learned over the years all this forethought tends to impair the communication. We need to get ourselves out of the way, our heads out of the way, and just speak from our hearts. It doesn't take long for people to look through you when you are saying something with genuine care and concern. They can feel it in your voice and see it in your eyes. If we follow the lead of the person we are serving, and get our expectations and fears out of the way, the words will usually come out the right way.

"I often say, 'There is no easy way to say this, but . . . I'm just going to say it . . . ,' when I am giving bad news.

"Most people are more resilient than we think. I believe we can convey our belief in the strength of that person, and empower them without candy-coating the news. We can offer to walk alongside them, letting them know what's involved in each step along the way. We can only offer our help as far as the next step goes, because we don't see the final destination. In a sense, we are only able to see a little ahead at a time, and can't see the whole picture. So, in giving bad news, talking about the near future, the next few steps, is more comforting than talking about the distant, more uncertain future."

Here are a few pointers to help communicate bad news:

1. Have your information right at hand. Sometimes we are the ones doing the hard job of explaining detailed or complex information to people in distress or to those we are serving as caregivers.

"Be ready for referencing and showing the person your facts and information. You need the verification right in front of you, ready for when the person asks questions and wants to see the 'proof' of the information with their own eyes. When people are hearing bad news, they often want to see where this news is coming from. It's not that they don't trust you, it's just that it helps things to 'sink in' when viewing the actual written materials. Having your information at hand conveys to the person you are organized (which helps them trust in you), as well as reassures them they are being included ('in the loop') of what is being assessed."

2. Say, "Here's what's going on so far." Lay out for the person what the latest reports are showing, and present the options for the next steps to take.

"Let the person know the plan, for example, what is proposed for a course of treatment, or what the options are for any path to take, with their pros and cons. In a sense, we are thinking out loud with the person, planning with and empowering the person. This 'knowledge is power' approach is comforting in itself, as it alleviates the person's fears of the unknown. Most people want to know 'how bad' or 'how serious' their situation is (say, if they are hearing about their lab test results after a biopsy), and we are there as interpreters to quantify the level of 'badness' in the results. We tell them 'how bad it is,' only taking one step at a time, one test result at a time. We need to be humble, and not jump to conclusions about the information. Offer phrases such as, 'This is what we know *now*, as far as we can tell.'"

3. Involve people you are serving in the decision-making.

"Show them the options for which course to take, but also offer them some time to think about it. Provide a follow-up plan for a check-in time, to take the next step."

❧ Jeff's Dos and Don'ts for Comforters

DON'T	DO
Cross your arms. Put your hands on your hips.	Let your arms and shoulders relax. This looks less threatening and friendlier.
Look down at the person.	Sit at eye level with the person.
Look distracted.	Look them in the eyes, especially when asking questions.
Talk in clinical or technical terms.	Talk in general day-to-day language (as you would your neighbor or friend).
Talk to an adult as if to a child.	Talk in general day-to-day language (as you would your neighbor or friend).
Keep talking.	Pause to check in with the person. Offer opportunities for clarification or questions.
Speak quickly, loudly, or curtly.	Speak in a lower voice, evenly. You can be emphatic and firm with a soft voice, too.
Ignore family members and friends in the room.	Acknowledge and greet family members and visitors in the room with the person.
Say you are sorry without meaning it.	Be genuine, speak in a sincere tone.
Tell a person to wait with no explanation.	Let them know why they must wait longer for something, or what time is involved. People are comforted when they know what is happening, rather than imagining all sorts of things going wrong. Taking just fifteen seconds to explain can make a difference.

• ❧ •

HONORING OUR HUMILITY

Adrienne Dormody, M.Ed., LICSW

Patient Education Specialist

Mayo Clinic, Rochester, Minnesota

It helps to remember that no one human being can ever see the entire picture in relating to another person or situation.

Core Comforting Qualities: Humility and Integrity

I first met Adrienne in 1996 at a women's spiritual retreat in Minnesota called A Gathering of Women, led by bestselling author Joan Borysenko (*Minding the Body, Mending the Mind*) and her colleagues. In a greeting ceremony at the start of the retreat, Joan had asked us to pick up a red rose (from dozens generously provided to us), then walk quietly toward a participant unknown to us, and hand it to them in silence. For some amazing reason, I felt guided to give my rose to Adrienne.

We quickly opened up about our reasons for coming to the gathering, and found we both were seeking spiritual comfort in order to heal our bodies. Adrienne had recently completed a grueling regimen of treatments for endometrial cancer. She had known in her heart that sharing her story with other women at the retreat would bring her a sense of peace. In the end, this act of sharing inspired all of us women. In sharing our stories of facing radical life changes without maps, manuals, or mentors, we celebrated together our courage as well as our humility. We had taken our leaps of faith in thin air, courageously enough, but we admitted our humility in having to take many tedious, little steps before and after our leaps.

Ever since our rose ceremony, Adrienne and I have been steady colleagues, helping each other to restore our dedication to our professions, preventing ourselves from suffering from the burnout of compassion fatigue. Adrienne has comforted me with her funny, feisty, yet compassionate responses to my life's predicaments, and has taught me the value of humility.

Her gift of humility so generously shared with me has been reflected in all of her professional roles. She worked as a clinical social worker for the psychiatry department at the Mayo Clinic for more than eight years, providing group, marital, and family therapy. She arranged discharge plans for patients from around the world and from all walks of life. For another eight years, she served as a counselor for the Nicotine Dependence Center at the Mayo Clinic, and helped implement a counseling technique called Motivational Interviewing, with the goal of engaging patients more actively in their treatment. She taught this approach to many other professionals after being trained in it herself. Before her years at the Mayo Clinic, she was a teacher, a family educator, and a program coordinator for an in-home elder care service.

She is now a patient education specialist at the Mayo Clinic. She plans, procures, and develops materials for educating patients about the prevention and treatment of illness and the promotion of health. Her challenge in this role is to serve as a reliable conduit between health care professionals and the educational needs of patients and families. It is essential that she be rigorous in the interpretation and dissemination of vital information going back and forth between many parties.

Considering the demands of being a primary liaison between the Mayo Clinic's vast systems, it's amazing how Adrienne brings forth her qualities of humility and integrity to establish and maintain reliable lines of communication. She can walk into an emotionally charged situation with a distressed patient, an anxious family, a frustrated nurse, and a harried physician, and diffuse the tension by being unassuming and attentive, asking simple questions and allowing all parties to clarify and specify their needs. In short, her humility helps her get herself out of the way so she can attune to others. Adrienne explains how she serves people at the Mayo Clinic:

> "To be comforting, it helps to remember that no one human being can ever see the entire picture in relating to another person or situation. I find it humbling and comforting that I can only see part of the big picture, only part of the whole truth. In working directly with patients, I've tried to walk into a room without assumptions and expectations, to be totally present to them. This has been hard work, as it does not always come naturally to me. I've had to keep in mind that my view, the physician's view, the nurse's view, the patient's view, and the family's view are all only pieces in the bigger picture. I have gained great respect for what physicians and nurses do, especially with all the demands

on them in these times. I believe they work extremely hard for their patients, though they see through their lenses, too, as we all do.

"In my role as patient educator, serving as a liaison between many health care professionals and patients, I need to be a comforting presence while listening to each person's vital input in order to put the pieces together. If my ego, or my tension, or my biases interfere, I cannot fairly convey important health information, and much could be lost in miscommunication."

Over many years, Adrienne and I have enjoyed our favorite, never-ending conversation about the importance of humility and integrity in our roles as comforters. We've discovered that true comforters can embrace the fallibility of themselves and others, as they understand how long-cherished beliefs can suddenly collapse in the chaos of a radical loss. Even our most sacred commitments and values can sometimes fall by the wayside in the turbulence of unforeseen changes. Because many comforters know very well how it feels when one's world falls apart, they can sit humbly and openly with devastated people who don't know what to believe anymore. Adrienne says:

"Absolute certainty is an illusion. Life can change instantly. We can think we have it all together, and then suddenly our world is turned upside down. A diagnosis of a life-threatening illness can do that to us. It happened to me

fourteen years ago, when I was diagnosed with endometrial cancer three months after my wedding. I was starting
a new life with a whole new family, full of joyous expectation. The resulting chronic issues challenged me to the
core. My pain and consequent humility from that experience has brought me to a deeper sense of compassion and
respect for comforting others and myself, and for educating
patients and staff in my work. I still believe that no one has
the last word on anything—at least, not for long!"

Recently, on New Year's Day, Adrienne and I tenderly
shared each other's list of resolutions for 2010, as we tackled
the same old goals we've been struggling with for decades.
In acknowledging each other's fallibility and lack of focus in
reaching some of our resolutions, we felt much lighter when
we declared we would honor how we handled the obstacles
and detours that had taken us off course. As always, when
I've panicked that I've lost my way and gotten off course with
what I was "supposed" to be doing, Adrienne has reassured
me that I'm a worthy person, whether off course or on course.

The Most Important Qualities of a Comforting Person

Adrienne says the following core attributes define a comforting person:

- humility
- warmth

- sincerity
- interest in others
- integrity

ADRIENNE'S COMFORTING PRACTICES
IN HER WORK

1. Smile and look people in the eyes.

Adrienne believes in the importance of smiling with our greetings. People feel instantly welcomed with our warmth and our friendly eye-to-eye recognition.

Smiling genuinely is a sure bet for the nonverbal language of comforting in the first five seconds of an encounter. We don't need to give big, gregarious smiles and warm and fuzzy welcomes, but kind, modest smiles of acknowledgment make a world of difference for people in distress.

2. Establish an alliance by making it clear what
our different roles are in serving the person,
including our role as a provider.

Adrienne suggests we assist the person in getting acquainted with us in our role as comforter, and further, by explaining how our role fits in with other providers and social supports. The art of acquainting people with one another is one of the finer arts of comforting. In the *Oxford Dictionary*, the word *acquaint* means to "make someone aware or familiar with."

People who step into busy, impersonal, or vast settings

can get their bearings sooner by having providers acquaint them to the particular roles they are playing, and how to utilize their help. We feel more empowered when we know the appropriate go-to people for assistance with our needs. People in distress need easy, concrete orientations to acquaint them to new programs, activities, or routines.

As comforters, we might accompany those in distress with "walk-throughs" or tours to new places where they will be receiving services. Or, for more social and recreational activities, we can accompany them in meeting new faces and getting them started with new connections. In short, comforters can be great navigators and tour guides for paving the way for people in distress to get acquainted with new connections and networks.

3. Ask people open-ended questions about their lives, and engage in talking about their interests and concerns.

Adrienne knows how to elicit conversation by finding topics of interest with the people she serves. She also has a pleasant, gentle curiosity about people's lives.

Again, as part of acquainting ourselves, asking open-ended questions invites much more conversation than questions with yes or no answers. A good comforter can hone in on what interests the person might have, saying things such as, "Sounds like you haven't missed an episode of *The Dog Whisperer* for years! What about the dogs in your life?" (Instead of asking, "Do you have dogs?")

4. Acknowledge the importance of everyone's roles.

Adrienne is able to respect and appreciate the many roles everyone plays in meeting the needs of those we comfort. Again, her humility serves her well in valuing how we each play a part in "seeing the big picture." Comforters are important for reassuring the person in distress how everyone is vital in the roles they play, from the ones paying the bills, to the ones doing the surgery, to the ones dumping the trash. We all matter in the world of comforting.

Adrienne's Suggestions for Caregivers and Families

1. Show people you care, by telling them, writing them, giving them something, offering your help.

2. Acknowledge and clarify your role as a comforter, and acknowledge the roles others play in caring for them.

3. Listen and attend. Be fully present. Smile. Look them in the eyes. (Though this is hard to do these days with so many things demanding our attention.)

4. Touch their hand or arm, or give them a hug (with their permission).

5. Show interest in what they are interested in. Ask questions about their specific interests.

6. Invite them for a meal or a cup of tea.

7. For families, sit down for a meal with no interruptions, just to enjoy each other. Have a real conversation, and listen to one another's stories (no cell phone talking, no TV on, no text-messaging).

8. Share with each other three things you are grateful for that day. (For children, this is a soothing activity right before bedtime.)

9. For children, play recordings of grandparents or loved ones telling a story. (I used to do this with my son when we lived far from his grandparents.)

COMFORTING THINGS FAMILIES CAN DO IN A HOSPITAL WITH SOMEONE WHO IS ILL

- Show up, be there with the patient, be reliable about visiting when you say you are coming.
- Act courteously and respectfully with all staff. (Which affects the patient's care.)
- Make use of the chapel or a chaplain. Or walk on the grounds, courtyard, or quiet spaces.
- Share amusements and hobbies (if appropriate—check with provider first) such as crossword puzzles, knitting, books, photos, board games, toys, magazines, crafts, gifts, flowers.
- Eat a meal together (if appropriate).
- Provide soothing touch (if appropriate—check with provider first). Rub their feet or hands, maybe add lotion.
- Provide music, entertainment.

✺ Adrienne's Dos and Don'ts for Comforters

DON'T	DO
Judge the person as good or bad.	Maintain a sense of humility ("There but for fortune go I. . . .").
Be distracted.	Center yourself before interacting with the person.
Multitask.	Focus your comfort on the person, and take one step at a time.
Act hurried.	Steady: Remember the purpose you are serving.
Interrupt.	Allow the person to complete their thoughts.

· ✺ ·

KEEPING IT REAL

Alicia Rasin

Founder, Citizens Against Crime

Victim's Advocate, City of Richmond, Virginia

Community Liaison, Richmond Police Department

Just show up, listen, keep it real, and be right there with them.

Core Comforting Qualities: Genuineness and Empathy

For the past twenty years, Alicia Rasin has devoted her life to comforting grieving families devastated by homicide, gang violence, and other traumatic losses such as suicide, fire, and domestic abuse. She guides families through the steps of organizing funerals, memorial services, and candlelight vigils, and follows up with visits for grief counseling. She advocates for families, and provides them with contacts and vital referrals to legal aid, mental health, and other social services. She trains police officers at the Richmond Police Department in how to approach and serve families traumatized by murder and gang violence.

Alicia loves her city enough to venture into neighborhoods immediately after a shooting, to reach households with her radiant compassion. She has even gone to homicide scenes before the police have been called. She is well known in Virginia for her courage and generosity of spirit, and has been named "Richmond's Ambassador of Compassion" by former governor Tim Kaine, as well as the "The Mother Teresa of Richmond" by former police chief Rodney Monroe.

WHEN I FIRST SPOKE WITH ALICIA on the telephone, she greeted me with a hearty hello and put me at ease right away. After I told her a little bit about this book, Alicia exclaimed, "People really don't get enough comfort. It's such a shame."

Alicia was remarkably open about her personal challenges with her health and well-being. She had survived stomach cancer years ago, and more recently had undergone heart surgery. She now volunteered as a victim's advocate and police liaison with the City of Richmond, living on her disability checks, still working full-time, in constant demand. "I'll probably need more heart surgery, too, my doctors tell me. I have a lot of heartache because I have a lot of grief, which is why my heart is having so many problems. It's mostly from losing my dad a year and a half ago. I still miss him so much."

Alicia had been her father's primary caregiver for many years, and he had died in her arms in late 2006. She still lived in the house where she was raised, surrounded by his belongings.

I asked if her work with grieving families throughout the Richmond community was stressful for her, given her heart condition and her grief, and she emphatically stated, "Oh no, no—the work I do giving comfort to people really *helps* my heart a lot. It keeps me going. I'm doing the work God wants me to do. Comforting people is what my life is all about."

In the fall of 2008, I finally had a chance to meet Alicia in person at her home in one of the oldest neighborhoods in Richmond, Church Hill. Alicia had a huge Christmas tree lit up with blue lights, standing tall and touching her high ceilings in her sunny living room. Across her rose-colored walls and tabletops were many affectionately displayed pictures of her friends and family, plus the faces of the many families she had served over the years.

We talked more about how hard it is for families and friends to find time to do comforting things with each other. Alicia related this problem to her own agenda of her busy weekend. "Today, I've got so much laundry to do, but I am trying to get out to see my friends who've waited to get together with me."

I agreed that it's sad that we have such a tough time putting time with our loved ones at the top of our lists.

"That's why, when we *do* finally get together, we need to be ourselves and give our hearts to each other. People need us to be all there with them, not just up in our heads. Our time together is so precious."

She spoke further about how we have been socialized to mask our feelings in our haste to make grieving people feel better. She laments, "If we don't keep it real, we only make them feel worse. Because grieving people feel different from us, we can help them by showing we feel some of their sadness, or anger or fear, so they don't feel so alone. They can feel us feeling with them, and that's a lot of comfort right there."

In our series of talks, Alicia has inspired me with her refreshingly honest and heartfelt observations about how we need to be ourselves when we offer comfort. Quickly feeling comfortable and open with her, I admitted that, even with my counseling training, there were times I lacked confidence in being authentic while consoling grieving parents. I'd never had kids of my own, and was worried that I might not be able to relate to mothers and fathers genuinely enough, from missing this experience. I felt a bit "different."

"Alicia," I asked, "how dare I try to know the pain of parents whose children have died?"

She surprised me with her tender response, "I never had my own kids, either, Val. But I've been working with grieving parents for over twenty years, just by feeling their sorrow. I let their sorrow touch my own sorrow—my sorrow about my dad who died, or my friend who is sick, or my community in trouble—real sorrow. We are all human, and sorrow is in all of us. It's okay if you don't always know what to do when someone is in pain, as long as you can say with all your heart, 'I am right there with you.' People will believe you care if you just show up, even if you don't have much to say. Just show up, listen, keep it real, and be right there with them."

Alicia told me that she learned how to comfort by watching the different ways people comfort each other. Ever since she was a small child, she noticed what makes people feel better. "I'm still learning every day what comforts people, and I allow people to show me how to comfort them. I think we need to get better at observing more, listening more, tuning in to the little ways we can comfort others—people give us signs for what to do. Too many people don't slow down enough to notice these subtle but important signs that tell us how to comfort each other."

Alicia heartened me, reminding me of our human, universal sorrow and pain, giving us the integrity and "credentials" for being comforting with each other, no matter how different our personal experiences had been. I remembered women like Alicia, though "childless" themselves, who gave themselves to the children and families of the world, like Mother Teresa, or other women in spiritual and compassionate service. Alicia's words reconnected me to this wider community of comforters. And I am forever grateful for the honest and generous time she spent with me.

ALICIA'S MOST IMPORTANT QUALITIES OF A COMFORTING PERSON

- Accepts going into a situation without knowing how it will turn out

  "We just don't know what's going to happen when we reach out. We need to let go and trust in something healing that happens beyond what we can control. It's really taking a leap of faith to comfort someone in great pain."

- Feels what someone else feels, even without understanding that person's experience

  "Just by remembering we are human, we can tap in to our common emotions through our hearts."

- Can see through a person's pain to his soul

  "A comforting person can see how someone is trying to cope with their pain. Comforting means seeing what they are doing to hold up, not just the distress they are in. We need to believe in that person and their own way of healing."

ALICIA'S COMFORTING PRACTICES IN HER WORK

Here is how Alicia comforts a family after a loved one has been murdered:

*"We gather to say prayers and
blessings out loud."*

"First of all, right after I walk in the door, I ask everyone to gather around me and I say a few words of prayer with them. We have a kind of prayer huddle, all the family members, and sometimes friends or neighbors. I let other people say their own prayers if they want to."

*"We hold hands in a circle, and share
our memories and feelings."*

"After our prayers, we stay in our huddle, and we all hold hands in a circle. I just listen to what people are saying and feeling about the loss."

*"We share hugs, if the children and
families give us permission."*

"If they feel like it, the young ones will come up to me and hug and hold me. The kids seem to like that, and they smile, reaching out to hug me. It's important that they have a choice to hug me or not. But most kids do want to give me a big hug. Some of those kids haven't hugged anyone in a long time, especially if someone has died in their family."

*"I check back on the family a few
days or weeks later."*

"Later on, in a few days or weeks, I go back on another visit to check in on the family. It really helps to bring young volunteers from other grieving families with me. It gives the family hope when I come with other teens who have also lost someone, and who understand what the new family is going through. The kids can talk to the kids while I can talk to the adults, and it works very well."

"We take more time to share stories and memories."
"When I visit families with the teen volunteers, it's important to take a long time for sharing memories and going into details in our stories. A lot of times we talk about something funny and have a really good laugh. Sometimes the humor brings people together, because everybody wants to add more to a funny story, and it helps to get all kinds of feelings out."

Alicia's Dos and Don'ts for Comforters

DON'T	DO
Cover up your sorrow.	Tell them how sorry you feel.
Worry about what you should say.	Just listen and follow what they say.
Worry you don't have enough in common with people in distress.	Open your heart and feel their pain.
Say, "I know what you are going through."	Say, "I'm so sorry you are going through this."
Ask them to call you.	You call them to check in.
See them, but not let them know when you are going to see them again.	Follow up, check in later.

• ❦ •

THE POWER OF OUR PRESENCE

Reverend Patricia Ellen, M.Div.

Outreach Director, Center for Grieving Children,

Portland, Maine

Abbess of the Chaplaincy Institute of Maine

> *When you give someone your total attention, you are creating a bubble of comfort, a little pocket of safety.*

CORE COMFORTING QUALITIES:
PRESENCE AND CALMNESS

As the outreach director at the Center for Grieving Children, Patricia oversees a program that reaches more than one thousand children and professionals a year, providing education and crisis support. When a school faces a death, crisis, or life-threatening illness, Patricia and the center's staff and trained volunteers appear on site to support and comfort children, staff, and parents. Patricia fields questions and advises staff on concerns such as how children can be involved in wakes and funerals, how teachers can assist grieving children in their classes, how parents can be supported by school staff, or how to mobilize crisis intervention teams. She coauthored the book *A Family's Journey: A Handbook for Living with Illness and Finding Hope.*

Patricia is also the abbess of the Chaplaincy Institute of Maine, a role that dovetails beautifully with her outreach director position. In her work as abbess, she supervises and

mentors chaplains in training to become interfaith minis-
ters. In both of her positions, she serves as a guide to an
individual's personal and transformative journey through
loss, the search for meaning, and spiritual growth. Patricia
explains, "Our journeys through grief as well as through
spiritual growth are processes fraught with turmoil, doubt,
and 'dark nights of the soul,' but they can also bring us gifts
of inspiration, compassion, and wisdom. Most chaplains have
been through significant losses in their lives, and conversely,
many people who have been through grief want to comfort
others eventually, and are called to serve in some way."

She feels blessed to be working with organizations that
value the importance of comforting the comforter, and practice what they preach with their own staff. "The staff at the
Center for Grieving Children will drop everything to stop
and be there for each other when we need it," Patricia states
confidently. "They support me in all that I do, as well as all
that I *don't* do to prevent burnout. Having true colleagues,
reliable fellowship, and kindred values are vital for me in
serving my community as a comforting professional."

P ATRICIA AND I, both morning people, are together at seven
a.m. for our breakfast meeting. Though we have a lot to
cover and I am tempted to grab my notebook, she sits back
in her chair with a relaxed smile, letting me know without
words there is no need to rush. Her calmness is contagious,
even in the fast-food restaurant on this Friday morning, where

the townspeople of Gray, Maine, are increasingly streaming in behind our booth. I enjoy my coffee, and Patricia asks if our meeting spot was easy enough for me to find. Her directions were perfect, I answer, and wait to see if she has that "ready" look to get down to business with our interview.

She easily glided into a conversation with me about our common interests in spirituality and counseling work. She described how her teaching, presenting, administrative, and facilitation duties sent her to many appointments at venues scattered all over southern and central Maine. Patricia shared that she would be working to 9 p.m. that night, a frequent requirement for her, although I could not detect a bit of stress about her day's itinerary. Working marathon hours just came with the territory of doing the work she loved. Like other highly comforting people I'd known, she could manage to be calm and friendly and appear unhurried on a very demanding day.

In our conversations about comforting, even when discussing the sad news of the deaths of a few students at some schools recently, I felt Patricia's serene acceptance of allowing people to grieve in their most natural ways. There were no right or wrong ways to grieve, and staff, parents, and kids were not to be judged for how they handled the unfolding crisis at their schools. Some teachers might have sought comfort in the teacher's lounge and stared at the walls, while others researched grief on the Internet. Some social workers might have hugged parents; some principals might have made fifty phone calls in an afternoon. Some kids had written sympathy cards, while others played softball. For Patricia, everyone was doing what they needed to do to grieve, and she was there at the school to quietly stand in the background, to listen and help them find what grounded them, focused them, made things feel a bit more normal. Patricia served in a ministry of presence, gently offering her full attention and unconditional caring to people struggling with strong and often unfamiliar emotions.

"When you give someone your total attention you are creating a bubble of comfort, a little pocket of safety. I call this sacred space. It's possible to make a bubble of comfort in the midst of a crisis at a school after a student's death, even in the hallways, just by walking and talking one-on-one with a child and being completely present.

"We can serve as comforters by dropping the 'to do' lists in our minds, and by following the lead of the person in need. Does that person want to talk or walk or draw or just sit under a tree with you? Does that child or that teacher need to ask you questions, or want you to hear them think out loud, or sit down with them to make a difficult phone call?"

Although Patricia is a phenomenally productive, busy, and accomplished person, sitting in her presence gave me a sense of serenity that lasted the whole day. She exudes a graceful trust in the natural flow of things, when we don't force things to work—especially things like emotions. She reminds me we can't drive our feelings at the same pace as our minds by our agendas, dreams, or even our best intentions. There is comfort in the presence of people like Patricia who always make time to listen to our feelings, and our stories.

I ask Patricia about her center's unique role in providing comfort for entire organizations.

"We can comfort an entire organization by comforting people one encounter at a time. Of course, it takes time, but there is a ripple effect, if you just keep showing up, steadily, quietly, in the background, making yourself present for the ones who privately seek you out. Families alone, as well as organizations alone, may not always be able to comfort themselves, when loved ones or coworkers are too busy coping to be readily available to each other. People from the greater community can be brought in to help hold them through the turbulence and loss. Our outreach program at the Center for Grieving Children comforts the caregivers at our schools, businesses, churches, and health care centers when they are too overwhelmed to be the comforters. Caregivers need the comfort first and foremost for themselves, and we can at least alleviate some of the fear and self-judgment they carry for not being comforting enough. By supporting staff this way, reassuring, guiding, and educating them, we strengthen their confidence as comforters."

Patricia again returns to the idea of there being a power in our mere presence when we simply make time to be there.

"I've learned a lot from the quiet, loving presence of my friends, especially after the death of my son. When people have offered their comfort without words, walking with me outdoors, or giving me a hug, or smiling and listening, I can feel their hearts speaking in sacred silence."

Patricia's Qualities of a Comforting Person

- Can be totally present
- Trusts and respects the other person's strength and wisdom
- Has an interest or curiosity in others
- Is able to listen deeply without knowing the answers
- Is open to knowing there is no single or right way to face loss

Patricia's Tips for Comforting Children

Many of the activities Patricia and her colleagues do in schools where a loss or crisis has occurred could be applicable in any situation where a child needs comforting. Following are the most important suggestions Patricia offers.

Quietly engage children in doing simple, hands-on activities.
According to Patricia, for children and teens dealing with new and strong emotions, doing easy, concrete projects can be grounding and calming. When adults join in the activity, they can gently begin a conversation with a child in a relaxed, casual way.

"When I assist with a crisis at a school (often with other staff and trained volunteers), I usually arrange a room with a varied assortment of easy activities. I will just sit quietly doing my hands-on project, and allow the children to engage with their activity, and later, gently ask what they are making with their hands, establishing a conversation. If they are comfortable talking with me, I check in with how they are doing that day.

"If they don't want to talk about their loss or their concerns, I let them know that it's fine if they need more time before they are ready to share. I provide opportunities to share thoughts and feelings around a loss or a problem, but that is all I do—offer the opportunities. Sharing is not a requirement for children or adults when they are grieving. I don't push children to vocalize their feelings or worries, and I remind them we do have a choice and a right to keep our feelings to ourselves if that feels best. We as adults need to respect their privacy as well as each other's privacy, and value their own timing for finding words for new and strange feelings of grief."

THESE EASY-TO-DO ACTIVITIES HELP CHILDREN FIND CHANNELS FOR TENSION AND DIFFICULT EMOTIONS:

- Writing, drawing, painting, or decorating cards that express support for those affected by the tragedy (i.e., the parents who lost children)

- Coloring or rubber-stamping pages of a scrapbook for photos and writings
- Doing beading projects to make as gifts
- Painting posters or banners to convey our caring thoughts
- Making a collage or a collection of collages, cutting images out of magazines to describe how we care
- Decorating a basket or cardboard box for letters, cards, gifts, or keepsakes

Provide one-on-one time or small group time.

Patricia says it helps to find quiet, private times with children to allow for them to offer their thoughts and feelings confidentially, such as when reading a story one-on-one, or taking a walk together outdoors. Children and teens often prefer to be away from other peers or siblings to feel private enough to share what is troubling them.

> "It's important to keep offering opportunities to share, as check-in times, and to create routines for these opportunities. This gentle acceptance and caring supports the griever in being patient and honest with themselves while handling confusing and unsettling emotions."

Keep as normal as possible the same daily routines.

Patricia says routines are comforting for all ages, especially for young children. Whether it's feeding the goldfish every morning, going to a Sunday matinee, or putting on our slippers after dinner, routines help us step into the present moment and connect with the world around us. Above all, routines help our lives feel normal during times of loss and change.

Tell the truth.

Children need to know what is happening and have an adult to turn to with their questions.

Play with them—join in with what they are sharing.

Children often play out what is concerning them as a way toward understanding what they are facing. Younger children can communicate with dolls, toys, stories, stuffed animals, drawings, or playing games to share what they are feeling and learning about the situation at hand.

Patricia's Advice for Parents Comforting a Child

Following is a list of Patricia's suggestions for parents or caregivers who want to help a child or children through a difficult time.

1. Snuggle under a special blanket together, when sitting together talking, reading, or watching TV.
2. Have regular family time.
3. Share meals together and tell stories.
4. Do bedtime stories and prayers together.
5. Perform little acts of kindness and caring for each other—small things go a long way.

6. Go outside to look at the stars and moon together, or just lie on the ground on a blanket and watch the sky (in the daytime watch the forms in the clouds).

7. Act out rituals of remembering, such as lighting candles or sharing memories around the dinner table.

8. Create sacred space, such as a spot in a garden, a shelf for keepsakes, or a wall for special pictures.

Patricia's Dos and Don'ts for Comforters

DON'T	DO
Try to fix "it" for them.	Listen closely, allowing for silences. Be curious.
Assume you know what is right for the other person.	Let the person lead with what they need—quiet, listening, help with something, diversion.
Tell them you "know how they feel" because of (your story).	Give them your undivided attention, put your own thoughts aside.
Rush them through their feelings. Judge them.	Let them safely express their feelings, tears, anger, and confusion as long as they need to.

· ❦ ·

THE MAGIC IN A CONVERSATION

Reverend Hal Wallof

Retired Presbyterian Minister

Eastern Virginia

I have within myself a core belief that this world, with all of its possibilities for failure, sickness, and death, is the perfect place to grow our souls.

Core Comforting Qualities: Generosity and Warmth

Since retiring from his twenty-two-year post as minister of a Presbyterian church in eastern Virginia, Hal Wallof has been what he calls "freelance." Busier than most "working" people I know, when he isn't sitting down with soul-searching seminary students, feuding neighbors, troubled colleagues, or compassion-fatigued members of a church, he's busy volunteering for Meals on Wheels or sitting on a committee for special education in the local schools. Hal also paints spiritually evocative pieces, often with angels as subjects, that have been featured in Richmond galleries and has extensive knowledge of the works of Carl Jung.

Over the course of the past fifteen years, Hal and I have met over coffee, hot chocolate, wine, nachos, or sushi, and he has graciously given me his time as a friend, an elder, a colleague, and a fellow "peaceful warrior." Hal is so warm, spontaneous, and easy to be with that I've opened up and expressed things to him that only my cat has heard. And, for every problem I've ever presented to him, whether or not the problem was resolved, I've always left our conversations feeling better. There is just a certain glow that comes from being in his unconditional presence. Being around Hal, I am reminded that some of the best comforters are our friends. Indeed, says Hal: "I hesitate to call myself a mentor, spiritual director, or counselor—even though I have had training in these areas. I prefer to be known just as a friend. In the context of friendship, I try to awaken the inner seeds of comfort which I believe are within us all. Behind this approach is a belief that we are all created in the Divine Image, and as such, have all that we need within ourselves. This divine inner reality, which includes the seeds of comfort, is accessed when people relate to each other in a mutual exchange of touch, conversation, silence—perhaps over coffee, lunch, or a simple visit in a peaceful place."

Hal's core qualities of warmth, kindness, and generosity as a pastor were his foundation for building trust and understanding with his congregants. Even as a young man, starting out his post, he inspired, motivated, and guided his congregation with his friendliness and genuine interest in people. But Hal's story had a surprising twist that drew my attention. During his first year as a pastor, a couple of prominent, long-serving leaders in his congregation who disagreed with his initiatives were threatened by his rising popularity and warm rapport. Hal says:

"These guys had it out for me. They couldn't wait for me to make a mistake and wanted me to fail. They intimidated me, but I had no idea how to stand up to them. I was not prepared to face these challenges as a pastor, as I had believed pastors were only supposed to act from their comforting qualities. As much as I wanted to emanate an affable and generous presence, I suddenly needed to convey more of a warrior presence, a 'Don't mess with me' presence to protect myself. I had a hard time trying to reconcile my comforting presence with my warrior presence, and I was deeply conflicted for years."

Wondering how other comforters have handled similar situations with difficult persons, I asked Hal how he finally resolved his dilemma.

"My first solution was to hide or suppress my comforting qualities around these adversaries, so they wouldn't take advantage of me. Guys can comfort their kids and be softhearted at home, but they have to hide this side of themselves at work and in public, more than women do, I believe. But hiding such a vital part of my true nature did not work very well in the long run. Finally I discovered the martial arts, particularly kung fu, and I learned how to ground and center my body and raise the energy (chi) through my body. I became certified in the energy work of Reiki I and II. My two years of intensive training changed my life, convincing me I could be both a comforting presence and a warrior presence at the same time—a kind of peaceful warrior. Now I can be keenly present, soft enough to be attentive and comforting, but also confident and dignified enough to be respected by others."

Hal can now stand tall and stand his ground without tough words, just by his energized presence. In short, he can speak softly and carry a big presence. "The more I feel conflict heating up with someone, the more I come to my calm center." He told me about a pivotal moment in which he saw the power of shifting energy away from conflict:

"A wise neighbor of mine was facilitating a meeting for a group of people who were getting tense and defensive over an unpopular topic. Dissension was heating up the room. He couldn't manage to elicit a better group atmosphere. He sighed and stared hopelessly through the window. Suddenly, as if inspired by the sun streaming through the trees, he suggested the whole group step outside to eat lunch—have a picnic. Somehow this idea clicked, and everyone left the stuffy room to walk and sit down on the lawn to eat sandwiches. The whole mood changed in the group, and people started sharing stories and jokes. Later, they were able to return to their 'sore subject' and find a solution.

"I learned from this experience how to be more in the moment, and not so caught up in my intellect trying to solve problems. We are often challenged beyond our know-how and our expertise. Being aware of our surroundings and each other, and tuning in to the little opportunities for comforting that arise, we can be guided by the many nonverbal cues that give us signs for what to do."

After undergoing bypass heart surgery years ago and finding his way to a more balanced lifestyle, Hal tells me that he is basically a happy man. He loves the simple joys of life: "Life doesn't get much better than that first cup of coffee you bring to your wife, or she brings to you, and that morning walk in the woods."

Recently I pinned Hal down on exactly why he thinks he's so content with his life; he laughed and replied, "I'm old

enough now that I don't have to prove myself to anyone anymore. I'm retired—that helps, but mostly, these days, I can
sit down with people without having anything to prove."

The more I thought about this, the more it sank in that
when we are being truly comforting, we aren't trying to
prove anything at all, either to ourselves or others. Comforting has nothing to do with proof. Our comfort comes naturally when our care for someone else is more important than
proving anything. And that's a beautiful relief.

HAL'S MOST IMPORTANT QUALITIES OF A COMFORTING PERSON

- Can embrace, or at least accept with some compassion, the
  shadow-side of ourselves
- Can see a human being in front of them, no matter how different from them they may be
- Can spontaneously give of themselves, and expect nothing
  in return
- Has been through any kind of pain or loss and learned compassion from it

Hal's Comforting Practices with Others

HERE ARE HAL'S THREE BEST WAYS TO GET A COMFORTING CONVERSATION STARTED:

- Find the right place and atmosphere.
  - The key is, the space needs to feel comfort-
    ing to the person you are supporting. The

right spot makes a big difference in providing a good connection, especially to help start a conversation. Certainly pick a quiet spot, as free from interruptions and distractions as possible. If you are indoors, sitting at a small table or booth with a warm drink and a snack can be comforting. Find a corner, a private nook, a tree, a bench.

- Get started with easy warm-up topics, undemanding, "no brainer" comments (the weather, the sports game on TV last night, good food, the traffic today, how the kids or the dogs are doing, something attractive, like a necklace that the other person has on).

  - This may only seem like "small talk," but most people need a minute or two to transition into the meeting space and settle into it a bit, before "getting down to business." If the person you are working with is very silent, just following the lead of the person is best, and allowing a moment of quiet.

- Instead of directly asking, "How are you?" let them know you have been thinking about them and wondering how they are doing. Then you might say, "How has this week been going for you so far?" Or, "How has it been going for you today so far?" Or, "How did the test go last week?"

- It helps to start with a limited time frame or simple frame of reference when asking someone how they are doing. When people are distressed or grieving, having a context that they can grasp easily is usually more comforting.

- Avoid probing questions and "why" questions.
  - People don't like to be pinned down, especially when in distress. The freer they feel, the more likely they are to offer information. In the art of comforting, asking a question means inviting conversation and not fact-checking.

SUGGESTED COMFORTING ACTIVITIES FOR
CAREGIVERS AND FAMILIES

- Have picnics, or just walk in a park and sit under a tree for a sandwich.
- Tell stories at the dinner table, even if they are not about yourself (movies, TV shows, news items).
- Read poetry and passages from books with each other.
- Share comics and jokes with each other, and put cutouts of comics on the refrigerator.
- Play with your pets together.
- Make food or drinks especially for each other—comfort food (though this might not always be healthy . . . sometimes a little goes a long way to feeling better).

*§ Hal's Dos and Don'ts for Comforting Conversation

DON'T	DO
Finish their sentences for them.	Listen to their complete thought.
Ask yes or no questions. ("Did you get the tests back today?")	Ask open-ended questions. ("What's going on with the tests this week?") This invites more conversation. "What's going on with . . . ?" makes a good start.
Ask "why" questions. Ask too many questions.	Allow the person to share their experience as freely as possible without probing.
Tell them they are repeating themselves (even if they are).	Often, stressed or anxious people will repeat themselves to "think out loud" or "let it sink in." It's important to allow them these repetitions and to gently listen and let them sort out their thoughts.
Answer your cell. Or stare at the staff. Or fiddle with your PDA.	Give your undivided attention. If you have to take care of something, kindly excuse yourself and briefly explain why.
Be completely quiet and still.	Calmly show you are listening and following what they are saying.
Raise your voice if they raise their voice.	Keep your voice calm.
Leave them "hanging" if not finished. Leave a conversation without a sense of closure or a plan to continue.	Offer a time to follow up and check back at a later date.

CHAPTER 3

When People Resist
Our Comfort

When Loved Ones Resist Our Comfort

COMFORT COMES TO US if we can soften a little, open a little, receive a little, but that's not easy when pain is gripping us. Even when someone offers their time, patience, interest, love, or listening skills, we might hold back. Some grieving people resist completely, perhaps feeling that their vulnerability is just too risky to reveal. Think back to a time when you were going through a hardship of some kind and others approached you to offer comfort. Were you too scared, confused, angry, proud, or overwhelmed to allow yourself the gift of comforting? When we understand our own barriers to receiving comfort, we are better prepared to be patient and accepting when we face the barriers of others.

My own personal experience has opened my eyes to how *un*comfortable we can be about receiving comfort, especially when we are starving for it. Sometimes, the more we need it, the more we hide our need, to the point that when someone offers it freely with no justifications, no agendas, and no keeping tabs, we get scared and suspicious. And it can be just as hard for the comforter to persist past this resistance as it is for the one in pain to open up and receive their comfort. Anxiety, self-doubt, and anger can fester when our gestures of comfort are ignored, questioned, or rejected. What are we doing wrong? We doubt ourselves and worry about what is wrong with us.

When our attempts at comforting someone we love are rejected, it can be incredibly painful. Nonetheless, it is quite common for persons in distress to view their closest and dearest ones as the *very last* people they want to comfort them. Too much is at stake. Sometimes it feels safer and easier for them to spend time with less intimate people like new friends, health care providers, coworkers, hairdressers, classmates, church members, or neighbors. They prefer to reach out to someone with whom they don't feel guilty about burdening, or seek others in support groups with common dilemmas, or relax with easygoing, undemanding old buddies. In the meantime, the loved one trying to offer comfort might begin to feel jealous or rejected that others less close have been chosen to give the tenderness and affection they long to give. What am I doing wrong? they ask themselves.

In the caregiver support groups I've facilitated, I've heard many stories of loved ones being pushed away. One woman in a group, jealous that her husband with leukemia had only confided in his physician, exclaimed with a well-known line, "What am I, chopped liver?" Feeling left out and unappreciated is especially hard for spouses, siblings, and adult children in caregiver roles, because they believe they are *supposed* to be the primary comforters. But, in the spirit of comforting, we need to be willing to give up our previous roles.

Grief, in all its forms, surprises and tries us, calls us to think on our feet, listen with our hearts, and go with our guts. We can accept our loved one's resistance to us when we respectfully support their unique ways of coping, their ways of "holding up." And once we have, we might find some satisfaction in knowing that we have fostered the courage, hope, and dignity they have needed for their long, difficult journey.

Facilitating the Comfort of Others

When we, as loved ones, are deliberately kept out of a comforting role by the person in distress, we can still facilitate care and comfort by letting go of our need to provide more immediate comfort and helping in other, more resourceful ways. We can still be a vital, supportive presence without expecting our loved one to be receptive to our gestures of comfort and, in doing so, lessen the pressure on them. When we "back off" a bit, we are really upholding their freedom, integrity, and privacy.

Support, according to the *Oxford Dictionary*, means to "bear the weight of." In our supporting roles, as facilitators, we can help to bear the weight of our loved one's distress, by serving to sustain a comforting environment and contributing to related activities and resources.

Being facilitators of comfort involves serving in a supportive role, sometimes in the background. We can be supportive in a wide variety of ways, such as organizing enjoyable activities, coordinating services, assisting in chores, and enhancing comforting environments.

My friend Morna, for example, served as a facilitator of comfort in the first few days of our visit when I was grieving after my divorce. Before I was ready to open up and talk soulfully with her, she followed my lead and supported me in activities I initiated, in pastimes and interests that felt "safe" for me. At times, she gently offered opportunities for talking more intimately, but was willing to accept my refusals and didn't take my resistance personally.

Serving as a facilitator of comfort also means accommodating *someone else* to be a comforter in a favorite activity with the person in distress. A particular companion, volunteer, or family member might be preferred for walking the dog, a game of cards, gardening, going to the movies, giving a foot massage.

If we cannot serve as comforters ourselves, we can graciously facilitate comfort in keeping with our loved one's interests. In the ever-changing and delicate art of comforting, we can take turns with each other. It helps not to be attached to our roles, our egos, our sense of importance, and step openly and unassumingly into the present moment.

Many caregivers and loved ones find themselves playing both of these vital roles, alternating frequently, but always dedicated to the mission of comforting.

ACTIVE COMFORTERS	FACILITATORS OF COMFORT
Giving hugs, affection	Giving them "space," respectful distance
Listening to heartfelt stories	Listening to everything else
Keeping confidences	Keeping routines
Providing one-on-one time	Providing time for assistance
Acting in the foreground	Acting in the background
Knowing the whole story, the diagnosis, prognosis, "gory details"	Knowing less, not always kept "in the loop"

When Colleagues Resist Our Comfort

Offering comfort in the workplace is highly important, but it can be a delicate process for many of us. We might feel especially awkward when reaching out to people who are not as close to us, as we are not as familiar with their ways of coping with grief or stress. Also, in professional settings where our livelihoods and reputations are carefully upheld, we tend to be more guarded and scrupulous about how we approach our colleagues or others in our community.

Recently, a few of my coworkers and clients have lost loved ones, all within a few months. I have attended funerals, written sympathy cards, sent flowers, handed out chocolates, dropped off baskets of little gifts, given hugs, and shared heartfelt remembrances at memorial services. Yet after doing these seemingly appropriate tasks, and going "by the book" with the etiquette of condolence, I admit that I have absolutely no clue how well some of these offerings have been actually received. The art of comforting is even more of a mystery when we are serving people we don't know well, and I still struggle spiritually to allow and accept the mysterious ways our comfort comes around and goes around.

Likewise, many of my friends and colleagues, as well as dozens of participants in support groups have lamented how hard it is to ever "know for sure" if what they did to comfort their peers really helped or not. And sometimes, unfortunately, we stumble upon situations where a coworker flat-out refuses our comfort. One support group participant shared how embarrassed she felt after giving a hug to a coworker who had just returned to work after a month-long bereavement leave.

"Sandra had seemed to be a 'huggy' type to me, as I had watched her share hugs with many coworkers over the years. I was there the day she got the phone call about the death of her sister from a car accident, and saw her hurry out of the building. When she came back to our office after being gone for a month, I welcomed her back and reached out to give her a big hug. She was absolutely frozen, and barely moved her arms when I held her. I was so embarrassed that I actually blushed, and quickly excused myself. I could hardly look her in the eyes, and she avoided looking at me. I felt so shocked at her response to my hug that I had to run out to my car in the parking lot to have a good little cry. I was especially surprised at myself for feeling so ridiculous and awkward. It took me a while to compose myself before I returned to my desk to work near Sandra. I respectfully allowed her some privacy, yet I felt so powerless."

Similar scenarios have haunted many of us, when we might have missed the cues of the person we tried to console, or blurted out a gaffe in front of our coworkers. And when, indeed, someone did resist our offer of comfort, we blamed ourselves for not doing the right thing. But it's heartening to remind ourselves that these very messy, difficult encounters of trying to comfort others can sometimes present an opportunity for a breakthrough, resulting in more closeness and trust. In the art of comforting, we need to allow for surprises and hidden blessings.

Back to the story about Sandra: Fortunately, weeks later, Sandra bravely sent her embarrassed coworker a lovely card thanking her for giving her a hug at a "terrible time" for her. From what I've heard since, these two coworkers still share a cubicle three years later and feel closer to each other out of this experience.

Based on what I've learned from employment assistance professionals (EAPs), human resources professionals, counseling colleagues, support group participants, and my own personal encounters, I can suggest a few thoughts to keep in mind when we face someone who resists our comfort at work.

Accept and allow the person in distress to respond
in their own unique way, even if they don't appear
to acknowledge your offer of comfort.

It's common for employees returning to work after a loss to brace themselves, and be on guard against revealing any lack of professionalism or lack of focus, especially when they need to concentrate on their work duties and get back up to speed. (And let's face it: In this economy, they might be afraid of losing their job if they appear less than proficient after being on leave for a while.) Also, they may be numb and drained from undergoing surges of strong emotions in private, and are not able to express themselves openly. It might be difficult for them to return displays of affection, show appreciation, or engage in conversation. And keep in mind that the coworker might not appear to be functioning in their previous, "normal" ways, as grieving people often struggle with memory, attention, and a lack of energy, motivation, and confidence.

It helps to pause and remember the coworkers or classmates who have accepted and supported you over the years, when you were going through your own rough patches in your life. What did these comforters at work or at school do to help you? Reflecting on this is one way we can consider how we can support and compassionately accept the grieving or distressed people returning to our workplaces after a great loss.

Even if your first offer of comfort is refused or ignored,
don't assume this is a final, permanent statement or
verdict about your relationship with that coworker.

It's important to keep the lines of communication open, by being patient, unassuming, and flexible, and occasionally offering small, reassuring gestures that you are thinking about that person. You might send a "Thinking of you" card a few months later. But, once again, give this freely with no expectations.

Avoid personalizing the experience of having
your comfort refused or ignored.

Step back and observe the needs of that person at this time, and try to learn from your experience, being as nonjudgmental with yourself as possible.

Increase your knowledge of the experience of grief,
or about the issues the coworker is facing.

The more you learn about the grief process, trauma, or serious illnesses, the more you can examine your difficult experience with that coworker from a wider perspective, and develop compassion and understanding.

Join in activities with other coworkers who are doing
things to comfort the person in distress.

You can add to what others are doing to reach out to the coworker, such as writing with others in a sympathy card, placing your homemade banana bread in a gift basket, or putting a picture into a thoughtful scrapbook the team is making. Sometimes opportunities to offer comfort as a group arise spontaneously and casually, when coworkers get together for lunch or coffee.

> *Find friends and confidants outside of work to share your*
> *feelings of disappointment, anxiety, or powerlessness if the*
> *situation with a coworker in distress continues to upset you.*

Some workplaces also provide EAPs, organized by human resources staff.

> *Learn more about what your workplace can do to support*
> *employees in distress or grief, or inform yourself about*
> *what other workplaces have done that works well.*

Following are some common, comforting practices and policies that many workplaces support:

- Giving coworkers and supervisors time off to attend funerals and memorial services
- Sending sympathy cards and flowers as a group or as individuals
- Providing food, food baskets, care boxes, or care baskets
- Offering thoughtful gifts or collecting cash
- Helping the employee by providing flexible hours or reduced workloads
- Assisting with transportation and other arrangements
- Making phone calls on behalf of the employee (with their permission)

- Providing time off and family and bereavement leave
- Providing opportunities for supportive listening, acknowledging the loss, and offering condolence from coworkers and supervisors
- Providing EAPs to counsel employees who are affected by the loss (usually organized by human resources managers)

As much as we'd love for all of our efforts at comforting to be instantly appreciated, it is often not possible for people going through extreme pain to anticipate our feelings as sensitively as we might hope. Therefore, it is best that the gift of comfort be given freely, with no expectation of receiving anything in return.

PART TWO

The Words *of*
Comforting

CHAPTER 4

Speaking Words of Comfort

FOR MANY OF US, the most difficult way to offer comfort is face-to-face—just sitting quietly and talking with someone in distress. In these intimate moments, we can get so hung up on trying to use the "right" words that we lose track of what it is we really want to say. But why is it so hard to administer this most vital form of comfort?

The Challenge to Comforting Language: A Hard World to Be Soft In

In this fast-paced world, it can be difficult to slow down and just "be there" for someone who needs us. We are so accustomed to all the "breaking news" about this "situation" or the other that stream constantly on cable television and on the Internet that our ability to comfort the people *right there* next to us can become compromised. Has all this instant communication decreased our patience and thoughtfulness for listening to grieving people who just can't seem to "get to the point" fast enough? Unfortunately, patience, one of the important qualities involved in comforting, is being tested across the globe. Yet it is patience that we need now more than ever.

It's not easy to find good role models for comforting conversation in our media. You just don't see a lot of comforters on television or hear them on the radio. Comforters are too compassionate to spar with the in-your-face people who appear on reality shows, and too unassuming to be on contests like *American Idol* or *The Apprentice*. And they are certainly not cut out to go one-on-one with those experts on "news" shows who point their fingers at us demanding that we "get over" our problems—who claim they "share our pain" but with a twinkle in their eye that hints at their disdain for our credit card debt, our joblessness, or our insomnia. No, if we want to learn how to inspire truly healing conversations, better that we train ourselves to tune out all this noise and listen to our hearts. This said, I believe that we can slow down a little when necessary to offer comforting words to those around us, and still make money, meet our bottom lines, stay with our itineraries, and keep on our schedules. The world won't come to a grinding halt just because we care enough to speak a more empathic language—even to ourselves.

What to Say and What Not to Say

As mentioned, many of us find that when we are face-to-face with someone who needs our love and support, we forget what it is exactly we want to express. It can be helpful to sit down in advance of your meeting to explore the key, meta message or messages you wish to communicate. Here are a few examples:

- I'm there for you. I'm available. I care.
- I'm listening. I'm following you. I'm with you.
- I'm interested in what you're telling me, and I'm willing to learn more from you about what you are going through.
- I'm feeling some of what you're feeling (sorrow, frustration), even if I personally have not been through what you've been through.
- I'm open, receptive, and I'm not going to judge you. I'm a "safe" person you can trust.
- I'd like to offer my assistance and my support with something specific.
- I would like to stay connected with you, beyond our meeting today.

These statements, or similar ones, express our desire to truly "be there" for the one in pain and, as such, are quite different from the words many of us default to when we're nervous or unsure of ourselves. When we feel uncertain about what to say, we tend to "default" to platitudes—the comments and sayings we've heard over the years from others—rather than speak in our own words and from our hearts.

Beware of platitudes! Our words can distance us from others, especially if they express that we think we know "what is best" for them. Devastated people in the first weeks and months of a loss or trauma can feel unheard, invalidated, or "preached at" by well-intended teachings and words of wisdom. Just listening and responding genuinely to what the person is saying is much, much more helpful.

Think back and remember the comments others may have said to you when they were reaching out to offer you reassurance or comfort. Did they or do they now strike you as insensitive or dismissive? Take note of these words and try to avoid them.

Over the past sixteen years as a support group facilitator many of the bereaved, traumatized, or gravely ill people I served have shared with me some of the statements others have made to them in their attempts to offer comfort as well as their "backfiring" effects. It's amazing when you think about it just how common these platitudes are. Following is a list of these common platitudes and suggestions for more helpful things to say to someone in need of your love and support.

🐾 "Be Strong" Platitudes

LESS HELPFUL	MORE HELPFUL
"God doesn't give you any more than you can handle."	"It sounds like this is really hard."
"What doesn't kill you makes you stronger."	"How are you doing with all this?"
"You need to be strong like your mother."	"I'm so glad you showed up here today."
"You need to be strong for your mother (for your children, family, coworkers)."	"I'm here, if you want to talk now."
"Be strong, and you'll get through it."	"I can only imagine how you've coped."

🐾 "Be Positive" Platitudes

LESS HELPFUL	MORE HELPFUL
"Something good will come out of this."	"It sounds like it's impossible to see what's ahead."
"It happened for the best."	"I'm so sorry this has happened."
"You are lucky that your father died peacefully."	"I was so sad to hear the news about your father."
"Be grateful it wasn't worse."	"You've had to deal with a lot all at once."
"You shouldn't be so angry."	"It isn't fair, is it?"
"Keep a positive attitude—it's better for your health."	"It's amazing to see you smile with all you are coping with."
"You're going to be just fine."	"I believe in you."

❧ "Be Faithful" Platitudes

LESS HELPFUL	MORE HELPFUL
"Keep up the faith."	"I'm thinking of you every day."
"This was part of God's plan."	"What has helped you get through the past few days?"
"This was God's will."	"I hope things get easier for you soon."
"God works in mysterious ways."	"I can offer my help, if you like."
"God tests our faith."	"It sounds hard, getting through these days."
"You need to pray more."	"I'll be sending you my thoughts and prayers."

❧ New Age Platitudes

LESS HELPFUL	MORE HELPFUL
"Your illness is the result of your negative beliefs."	"You must have been shocked to get the diagnosis."
"Your soul chose this tragedy before you incarnated."	"You need a break for a change."
"This is your karma."	"This stinks, doesn't it?"
"Your fears have made your chakras imbalanced."	"How is your body dealing with this strain?"
"The answer lies within. Peace lies within."	"I hope you can find some moments of peace."

🍃 "Get Over It" Platitudes

LESS HELPFUL	MORE HELPFUL
"It's time to put this behind you."	"This might take time."
"You need to keep busy, and get back to work."	"I believe you'll know the right time to return to work."
"You have your whole life ahead of you."	"Allow some time for this."
"Just think how you'll be doing by this time next year."	"Take all the time you need for yourself."

Other Helpful and Less Helpful Statements

🍃 "I Understand" Comments

LESS HELPFUL	MORE HELPFUL
"I understand how you feel."	"I can only imagine how hard this must be."
"I know what that's like."	"Do you mind telling me what it's like?"
"I went through a tough time like that, too."	"Tell me more, if you like."

Comparison Comments

❧ "Some Have It Harder"

LESS HELPFUL	MORE HELPFUL
"Just think of what the Hurricane Katrina survivors have been through."	"You already had enough on your plate."
"You should feel lucky. What you are going through is nothing like what my mother's generation went through."	"I'm so sorry you're going through this."
"Your problem is not as bad as what my son is going through with cancer."	"I am so sorry this has happened to you."

❧ "We All Go Through It" Comments

LESS HELPFUL	MORE HELPFUL
"We all face these hardships at some point."	"You certainly didn't deserve that."
"You aren't the only one going through tough times."	"Do you feel alone going through this?"
"This is a part of life, part of living."	"No one should have to go through that."
"Sh-t happens—that's just the way it is."	"This is really crappy."

🐦 "You Can Always Get a New One" Comments

LESS HELPFUL	MORE HELPFUL
"You can always get married again."	"Remember, I'm there for you as your friend."
"You can always adopt a child."	"You've tried so hard. . . . I'm so sorry."
"You can always have another child."	"It sounds like nothing will be the same after this."
"You can always get a new puppy."	"It must be hard living without your pet now."
"There are lots more fish in the sea."	"I'm sending you my warmest wishes for a bright future for you."

🐦 "Call Me When You Need Me" Comments

LESS HELPFUL	MORE HELPFUL
"Let me know if I can do anything to help."	"I can bring you some groceries this Saturday."
"When you feel ready, just give me a call."	"I'll call you Monday night and touch base."
"When you feel like socializing again, I've got a fun dance group you can come to."	"Would you like to come to my folk dance group with me next month on the twentieth?"

❦ "You Already Said That" Comments

LESS HELPFUL	MORE HELPFUL
"You've already said that three times."	"It sounds like this is important to you."
"Stop repeating yourself."	"This sounds almost too big to sink in."
"I heard you and I get it already."	"I hear you."

❦ "You Need to" Comments (Or "ought to" or "should")

LESS HELPFUL	MORE HELPFUL
"You need to get more exercise."	"Would you like to go on a walk with me?"
"You should go to a support group."	"Have you ever thought about a support group?"
"You ought to read . . . , and learn how to . . ."	"What have you been reading recently?"

❦ Asking "Why" Questions

LESS HELPFUL	MORE HELPFUL
"Why didn't you leave sooner?" (From your bad job, abusive spouse, approaching hurricane . . .)	"Sounds like you were going through hell."
"Why didn't your sister call you sooner?"	"I'm sorry to hear no one called you in time."
"Why didn't you stop smoking when you found out about the blood clot?"	"I can imagine it's hard to quit old habits."
"Why do you think God is putting you through this?"	"What you just told me sounds outrageous."

Beginning the Conversation

Often when we visit someone who is going through a terrible time it can be difficult to encourage them to share with us what they are thinking and how they are feeling. Sometimes just sitting with them quietly is what is needed. Other times, you may sense that they want to talk. Here are a few suggestions for beginning a healing conversation with someone who might be ready to engage with you:

- Verbal invitations to comforting:

  "I'm wondering . . ."

  "It sounds like . . ."

  "How have the . . . (lab tests, job interviews, dates with Jen) been going lately?"

  "What's been happening with the . . . ?"

  "I can only imagine how hard it is . . ." (Instead of saying, "I understand.")

  "What's been helping you get by these days?"

  "Do you feel like talking about it today?"

Once you have initiated the conversation, it is important to let it run its course naturally—don't force it. Take a look at the following list of common errors we comforters tend to make that halt the conversation when this is precisely what we don't want to do.

- Verbal barriers to comforting:

    Giving advice

    Interrupting long silences

    Changing the subject

    Asking probing, "why" questions

    Asking too many questions

    Asking only yes or no questions

    Preaching, lecturing, pep talks

    Overinterpreting

    Talking too much about yourself and your own
  "similar" experiences

    Talking too fast

    Talking too loud or too high-pitched

    Telling the person that they are repeating themselves

    Telling the person they don't need to explain some-
  thing to you that you already know a lot about

    Sounding clinical, technical, authoritative, smarter,
  or just plain bored

Hopefully, having looked over the contrasts between these less helpful and more helpful phrases and common barriers to conversation, we can clarify our own messages as comforters. Yet we need to keep in mind that our communication is essentially 80 percent nonverbal—our tone of voice and the expression in our eyes can say a lot more than any words we speak. Just the way we look at someone, beholding them with our gaze, speaks volumes about how much we care. Following are some ideas for sending nonverbal signals that will indicate to the person in distress that you truly care.

- Nonverbal invitations to comforting:
    Eye contact at the same eye level
    An occasional gentle smile
    Softly nodding the head at times
    Gently showing interest and caring
    Shoulders down
    Arms unfolded but comfortable and relaxed
    Listening for long stretches of the person's story without interrupting
    Being seated comfortably, tuned in, but not reclining
    Sometimes leaning forward slightly

If genuine, it's sometimes helpful to empathically reflect back to the person a gesture they made, such as shaking our head in disbelief with their disbelief, or a shrug of our shoulders as they shrug, or sighing with them when feeling the depth of their grief. (But if this is not coming honestly from us, these mirrored gestures will look awkward.)

- Nonverbal barriers to comforting:
    Taking notes (sometimes in a professional setting this may be necessary but still try as much as possible to maintain eye contact)
    Watching the clock or looking at your watch
    Doodling

Not turning off your cell phone

Answering your cell phone or texting

Looking distracted—looking down, looking up, looking around . . .

Looking for something while the person is talking

Rigid posture, shoulders up, and too tense

Eyes not at the same level as the person in distress

Arms folded

Hands on hips

Sunglasses on (move to a shaded place)

Fidgeting or rocking

Playing with your hair

The language of comforting is a language like any other— it can be learned but, once mastered, can become as effortless as breathing. And if our words and gestures are warm, empathic, and respectful, they will help to create a safe space for the comforter and the one being comforted to inhabit.

CHAPTER 5

Writing Words of Comfort

COMPOSING A COMFORTING PIECE of writing can be a sensitive and thoughtful process but can also, at times, be easier than speaking directly. When we write a letter or e-mail to someone in pain, we can take our time and reflect on what words we are choosing. Introverted people especially may find the gentle and private act of writing more meaningful. And indeed, a simple note written on a lovely card, perhaps with a soothing image on it, can serve as a keepsake for the person in need, providing them with comfort in the thick of their sadness and for years to come.

I have listed below an easy step-by-step guide to composing a comforting note or letter, be it for snail mail or e-mail. Most of these steps listed below apply to all kinds of comforting, not just for offering condolence for bereavement situations, but for supporting others at difficult times in general.

1. First, let the person know you have them on your mind.
   "Since I heard the news, I've been thinking about you every day."

2. Next, let them know how you feel.

   "It really took me by surprise at first, and now I feel so sad about your loss."

3. Then, ask how they are doing.

   "I've been wondering how you were doing this past week especially."

4. Let them know what you notice about any positive ways they are coping.

   It's often empowering for people in distress to have someone spot a strength or skill they are currently using, even at difficult times. As a friend, coworker, or family member, we might point out a particular quality to let them know we believe in them (though we would not want to dismiss their current level of pain and distress).

   "Carla, this might be the hardest time you have ever gone through, but I can't help noticing how good you are about returning all those phone calls. I don't know how you do it."

5. (For bereavement situations) If you knew the deceased, you can offer to share a memory about that person, or make a statement about what that person meant to you. Sharing briefly a significant moment of being with the deceased can help the griever feel a sense of continuity and connection with the people the deceased cared about.

   "Keith was one of the kindest people I ever met. Once he offered to call his former employer to help us locate a doctor for our daughter."

6. Express your desire to stay in touch and follow it up with a concrete offer of your time. Suggest a phone call,

a visit, an invitation to an activity, or an e-mail to check in later.

"I would really like to be there for you in any way I can. Would you like to join me next week for lunch at Joe's?"

7. Stay in touch.

Your letter is only the first letter, the start of a comforting process. Keep writing and checking in, for many months or longer. Especially pay attention to anniversaries, holidays, and birthdays, as these are times when people need extra support. In my work facilitating grief support groups for sixteen years, a common lament I've heard from grieving people is the silence that ensues after the first few weeks of their loss. After getting dozens of sympathy cards, flowers, gifts, food, and letters of condolence, there is little follow-up by many well-wishers some months later. They seem to drop away and move on. Some bereaved people are particularly sensitive to the lack of inclusion in other people's daily lives. This is why, when it comes to writing letters of condolence, we need to offer ways to stay connected and to keep sharing ourselves.

A Word of Caution

In writing a letter, as opposed to speaking with someone directly, we are given the opportunity to carefully review our words. Read and reread your letter or note to be sure that you have not inadvertently included any platitudes. In the previous chapter, I provided lists of commonly used platitudes and alternative things to say that will perhaps be more helpful to the person you wish to comfort. Many of these hold true for the written word as well, so you might want to review them on pages 111 to 113. Following are some platitudes that people tend to revert to in written communication in particular. Be careful to avoid:

Including cheery upbeat news from your own life.

It can be tempting to, in a "look on the bright side" vein, pad your letter with "positive" news from your life. Better to just focus on the person you're writing to and the pain that they are going through.

Instead, you might write: *"It sounds like this might take a long time to get through."*

Assurance that you "understand" what he or she is going through.

Instead, you might write: *"Please feel free to write or call if you want to, because I honestly would like to know about your experiences."*

Writing "We all go through it" comments.

Instead, you might write: *"With all you've gone through this year, your loss seems to come at a terrible time."*

Writing pages and pages of "helpful" thoughts and reflections about loss and grief.

Instead, it's better to keep your letter one to two pages, with simple, personal, and genuine words. Usually grieving and distressed people are not able to focus on reading a lot of text at one time. Though soothing words of wisdom from a self-help book or from religious scripture may have helped you, these words might not be helpful in the raw stages of grief someone is enduring.

Sharing Photos, Keepsakes, and Memories

Added to your letter, it can be heartening to send a photograph of a treasured moment, a card, an image, or a keepsake/souvenir from a favorite activity. A short poem, lines from a favorite song or book that the grieving person has shared with you in the past can be included, because what you have in common can be a comfort to that person.

A Sample Letter, Sent Inside a Card–
Supporting a Bereaved Friend

Dear Lynne,

You have been on my mind a lot these days. How are you doing? It must be so hard living without Jamie. I wish I didn't live 900 miles away, as I'd really like to see you. But for now, I was wondering if I could give you a call next Sunday afternoon, June 12th.

Yesterday on the radio I heard a song by Cat Stevens, "Moonshadow," and remembered how much Jamie loved that song back in 1972, when we all went to hockey camp. I remember how we sang "Moonshadow" together on one bright moonlit night, in that huge Buick station wagon when we drove back from camp. I was inspired, after hearing the song, to go through my albums in the attic, and thank goodness, I found this GREAT PIC of all of us at camp! I wanted to share this with you, and I hope this can be a keepsake for you.

I have you in my prayers every night.

Love,

Annette

A Sample Short Note, Sent with Pink Roses—
From a Husband to His Wife (during a painful wait
for their child's heart valve surgery and recovery)

My Dear Emily,

It's strange using words to express what I feel sitting with you all these hours in this sterile hospital environment. I haven't been able to find any decent words to comfort you. With these lovely roses, I want you to know what has been hard for me to say in the hospital—but here's what my heart wants to say:

You have been so patient with Julie, with the nurses, with the docs—and, mostly, with me. I know Julie feels your patience.

You have been so loving to Julie, to everyone, and me. I know Julie feels your love.

You have been so brave with Julie, with everyone, and especially with me. I know Julie feels your courage.

I never cease to marvel at how beautiful you are.

Let me hold your hand a little longer for this afternoon,
until we get the final news.

> *Your adoring husband,*
> *Matt*

Electronic Comforting

These days, many of us send our comfort electronically. We e-mail our comfort to loved ones, friends, and colleagues. The exact words chosen are extremely important in our cyberworld of comforting, as we don't have the facial expressions, voice intonations, eye contact, human touch, or even the tactile feel of our personal stationery or a beautiful card to express our comfort or condolence. On the other hand, electronic comforting allows those we wish to comfort to feel the immediate benefits of our act of reaching out to them.

Another benefit of electronic comforting is that we can follow and "stay close" to someone more easily—day by day or hour by hour—without intruding on their privacy (they can either chose to read our message or not, depending on how open they are feeling to our comfort). With a quick e-mail or text message we can:

- Check in with someone to let them know we have that person on our mind. *"Been wondering about you . . ."*

- Let them know we care about them. *"As your friend (sister, nephew, fellow band member), I've stopped to think about what you're going through this week, and what might be helpful."*

- Let them know we are feeling with them (empathy). *"I'm sad to hear you have just gotten such rotten news. I'm home tonight, so I can call you if you like."*

- Gently follow their progress and offering our support. *"I'm checking in again about how the meeting went with your brother . . . hope you landed on your feet."*

- Offer an "appointment" for more direct contact. *"Would you like me to call you next weekend? If not, that's fine–just letting you know I'm here."*

A Sample E-mail Letter–
A Brother's Support for a Bereaved Brother

Lee,

Last night, I had you on my mind. I was thinking about our meeting last month in Orlando, and wondered how things were going. From what you told me, it sounded like you had some rough weeks. I'm really glad to hear how the support group has helped you. I think it took a lot of guts to start going to that group. Considering you didn't know anyone in the group, it seems you fit in pretty well. I imagine that being with people going through the same thing is empowering. But also, I guess, it could be a drag, too.

I was talking with my friend in Orlando, Martin, last week, and he invited you and me to come down this winter,

*on January 30, for some R and R while his friends are in
town for a 20-year high school reunion.*

*I'll give you a call this coming Saturday morning and see
if you can make this trip.*

*By the way, I found this amazing picture you took of a
hawk a long time ago. You are pretty good with bird shots.*

Take care,

Tim

It's important to emphasize that in our role as comforters, it's better not to pressure the person in distress for a
response. We might ask them a question, but also let them
know they don't have to answer it if it doesn't feel right at
the time. For example, we could say, "I'm concerned, but
I realize you may not be able to get back to me yet. Just letting you know I'm standing by. Hope you take all the time
you need."

It's also good to show appreciation and humility if they
share personal information about their progress (medically,
emotionally, spiritually), and if they respond to our gentle
offers of more contact (a phone call, a face-to-face visit).

Here is a close friend reaching out to another after hearing she had a uterine biopsy in the past week.

First e-mail, October 18, 10:05 a.m.:

Checking in to see how you're doing since the biopsy. Sounds
like it'll take more days to get the results. Darn—what a wait!
I'm there for you with all my heart!

Second e-mail, October 18, noon:

> I'm free tomorrow night after 7 p.m. if you want me to call you. Really would like to talk with you soon, if it's okay with you. Always good to hear your voice.

Third e-mail October 18, 1:15 p.m.:

> Sorry we can't talk tomorrow on phone—you've got a lot on your plate. I've got you in my prayers in the meantime.

Fourth e-mail, October 22, 6:32 p.m.:

> Heard the biopsy results yet? I've got you on my mind and in my prayers.

Fifth e-mail, October 22, 8:02 p.m.:

> Thanks for getting back tonight. So they want more tests? Sounds like more waiting—really sucks. If you feel up to it, we can talk tonight—up to 11.

Sixth e-mail (upon hearing the unfortunate news that the biopsy and tests revealed cancer), October 24, 5:12 p.m.:

> What bad news. I know there is a lot to sink in. I am sending you a big hug with all my love. I'm standing by.

Seventh e-mail, October 24, 6:00 p.m.:

> Yes, love to talk with you tonight. 8 p.m.—great. Honored to be your friend at this awful time. Thanks for reaching out to me.

The friend is now willing to engage in a phone call with this comforter. Yes, the e-mailing has been softly persistent, and certainly not pushy. The e-mails have shown caring and affection, but not with expectations or demands for any news or personal information. We need to be balanced in our e-mails, as we "follow" people in a caring way, without hounding them for updates when they are already swamped in demanding or overwhelming circumstances.

THOUGH IN OUR SOCIETY today we resort more frequently to electronic communication, we need to remember the written word is only one, very limited, way of offering our comfort. Best of all, a face-to-face encounter brings forth all of our communication abilities, and greatly enriches our comforting messages and heartfelt reassurance of being there for that person. People in distress dearly need our direct contact, sometimes our loving touch and affection. In short, texting our comfort, though helpful, cannot be a substitute for our more sensitive, gentle, and finely attuned nonverbal language of comforting. Humans are, after all, "hardwired" for softness from each other.

PART THREE

*

The Comfort *of* Art

Inspiration from Healing
in the Arts

CHAPTER 6

Art as a Source of Comfort

Introduction: When We Run Out of Comforting Words

WE'VE ALL HEARD THE SAYING "A picture is worth a thousand words." When it comes to comforting, I'd say that art of any kind is worth a million words. Sometimes a beautiful photograph, the soft tones of a guitar, a joyous painting, or a tender scene in a movie can speak far more powerfully than any comforting words we might offer someone in need of our support.

One night, exhausted after a twelve-hour day of intense social work with clients, I plopped myself down on my sofa to watch the television reality show *So You Think You Can Dance*. That night, to my surprise, a couple brilliantly danced an emotional, poignant story about a woman with breast cancer and her loving partner. Having worked closely with cancer survivors over the years, and having recently lost a friend to this dreadful disease, I was deeply touched.

And I was not alone in my feelings—the whole panel was in tears, as were many people in the audience and, I suspect, millions of viewers around the country. In just minutes, the dance had expressed all the raw and conflicted emotions, as well as the delicate, loving gestures between loved ones facing life-threatening illness. In the days following the broadcast, I was heartened to stumble across several articles and blogs—many of them written by cancer survivors and their loved ones—indicating just how many people had been touched, comforted, and amazed by this gift from the dancers and the choreographer. And this is what art can do—it can help us to both express for ourselves and share with others our thoughts and emotions around a difficult life experience.

When we witness an artistic creation that contains the agony as well as the joys of being human, it shows us that we are not alone. For example, a cancer survivor told me how blasting Beethoven's Ninth Symphony into his bedroom had gotten him through the dark nights of his soul, as he joined with Beethoven's soul through the eternal language of his music. I also know an injured veteran of the Iraq War who pulled through grueling physical therapy while listening to the gritty rap of Missy Elliott's "Get Ur Freak On." And I've heard three different depressed, suicidal men share with me how Andy's "get busy living" determination in *The Shawshank Redemption* changed their lives.

The Comfort of Being
in an Audience

One frigid day in January 2009, I sat in the warmth of my home reviewing my checking account balance, which seemed to be plummeting as fast as the temperature outside. It was -1 degree F and falling and the wind was rattling my window as the arctic air slapped hard across the rocky Maine landscape. Clients were late in their payments *again*, so I was late in paying my bills *again*, but I found myself sighing with a strangely comforting sense of connection with all the other people on the planet in the same boat. The nearly bankrupt country of Iceland had much in common with me this evening, as did the General Motors workers, the workers from England to Russia to Singapore, all feeling the pain. Alas, I quipped to myself, what doesn't come around doesn't go around—money, that is, for most of us. My trusty little heat monitor, half filled with propane, hummed steadfastly, noisily, keeping my studio apartment warm enough, as long as I wore my fleece top over my turtleneck and jeans. At least I could pay my heating bill, but not much else.

Meanwhile, it was Golden Globe and Oscar season, and one of my great comforts, no matter how gloomy the weather, the economy, or my mood, was watching all the nominated films. Even with only twenty bucks to get me through a couple more days, and the matinee ticket meant living on rice and freezer-burned Lean Cuisines, movies were my soul food. I pulled on my boots, bundled up in winter wraps, heated up the car, scraped the ice off the windows, and headed down the interstate against the snow squall to the theater to lose myself in New Orleans, India, Germany, or San Francisco. For all the Oscar nominees, the lines were long and the theaters were packed.

As our economy grinded to a halt in the fall of 2008, going out to see movies quickly became a comforting activity for Americans, with box-office numbers increasing by 16 percent. In his article "Riveting Tales for Dark Days," David Carr of *The New York Times* noted, "When people fear for their futures, they like to gather in a dark room and stare at a screen, holding hands against the gloom."

Indeed, what else could drive people to leave their cozy homes on a dark winter's evening to wait in line, huddling in the cold, to buy a movie ticket and then to sit humbly in the darkness with a bunch of strangers to witness someone else's plight on-screen? There is something deeply familiar and comforting about being in a live audience as a story unfolds in a film, a play, or an opera. Being part of a chorus of laughs, sighs, gasps, and tears is a unifying event that brings us together in so many ways. We may never know who sat in the darkness with us, but for two hours, we rooted for our characters to triumph over their adversities, while putting our own adversities on hold.

Identifying with the Underdog

Of all the audiences I joined that winter, the one watching *Slumdog Millionaire* was the most animated and audibly responsive (both positively and negatively) of any I witnessed. A sea of curious New Englanders, we drifted together through the darkness into a balmy, colorful Mumbai. Along with the gasps, laughs, and hushed tension of a riveted audience, I harbored a hundred conflicting emotions and sensations running with the kids along train tracks, sewers, trash heaps, more trains, tunnels, the steps of the Taj Mahal, glitzy hotels, brothels, and humongous skyscrapers towering over ever more trains and bustling crowds. My circuits fast overloading, I could hardly breathe or think. Some scenes forced me to avert my eyes. Several audience members walked out. For those of us who hung on for the inspirational ending, we were treated to a joyous Bollywood dance, among even more trains. The audience broke into applause and cheers, and some hooted and gyrated in their seats. I marveled that these sensible, stoic New Englanders, more reserved than most Americans, had been so moved. People looked dazed, some exhausted, some smiling as they streamed out into the lobby. It had been an intense, rough ride, but most hardworking, hearty Mainers could identify with this gritty tale of a terribly deprived but extremely determined underdog.

No matter where we live, who we pray to, or who we

work for, it is extremely comforting to root for the underdog. We did it for Seabiscuit, the racehorse, winning for us during the Depression in the 1930s. We listened to *Rin Tin Tin*, the wonder-dog war hero, on the radio. We did it for *Rocky* in the late '70s. We rooted for Erin Brockovich, Antwone Fisher, Billy Elliot, Andy in *The Shawshank Redemption*, the *Whale Rider* girl, and Johnny Cash in *Walk the Line*. Even our latest, coolest *Star Trek* featured an underdog Captain Kirk. Fiction or true story, they gave us hope, telling us, "Get busy living or get busy dying" (*The Shawshank Redemption*), "Jai Ho" (*Slumdog Millionaire*), to "boldly go where no man has gone before" (*Star Trek*). And of course, "No man is a failure who has friends" (*It's a Wonderful Life*).

When groups of us root and hoot together with hope, whether in a darkly lit theater, in front of a football game in a friend's living room, or on Facebook, we give and exchange comfort with each other in enjoying the given art form, opening our hearts all the more in our sharing of the experience. This communal spirit of sharing our feelings and soulful expressions can carry us through bleak and frightening times, when stock markets plunge, when we lose jobs and homes, when we feel disconnected from our family members or from our own courage. No matter what is happening in our lives, the arts wait for us—a living spirit of hope and connection.

The Arts Teach Us
How to Be Comforting

Art calls us to stop, to pause and step out of our own personal dramas, and experience someone else's life—vicariously. According to the *Oxford Dictionary*, the word *vicarious* means "experienced in the imagination through the feelings or actions of another person." Art takes us through the ups and downs on someone else's journey and, as such, invites us to feel the empathy that is so vital to good comforting. Well-told stories—be they told in a book, a movie, or a beautifully drawn landscape as seen through the eyes of the artist—teach us how to walk in someone else's shoes, to identify with someone else's challenges. When we allow ourselves to be moved by art, we are opening ourselves to being inspired and nurtured by a greater sense of humanity.

Another way that art can teach us comforting skills is through the scenes it so often depicts of human connection—be it a random act of caring, a merciful gesture, or a heartfelt, honest confession. One simple yet brilliant example of someone offering comfort to another is in the movie *Little Miss Sunshine*, when the little sister, Olive, goes to comfort her distraught teenage brother who has run off from the family and is sitting alone in an empty field. Little Olive walks softly toward him, then quietly sits down next to him and reaches her arm around his shoulders. She just holds him in silence, without trying to convince him to join the family.

Quite soon, touched by her kindness and love, her brother feels better.

One of my favorite lessons about the art of comforting was learned from the movie *Leaving Normal*. In this movie we witness a bold, honest friendship between two women radically different from each other. I was struck by their peculiar bonding when they each ranted about how hard life had been for them. They angrily brought up the "make lemonade out of lemons" platitude, then quickly tore it to shreds with "What happens when life only gives you *shit*?" They pondered bitterly over what anyone could make out of shit, sans lemons, yet in all their bitterness, a sweet, soulful moment of connection suddenly occurs. Their mutual, fiery rage at the world actually burns away their fear of trusting and connecting with each other.

In short, art doesn't only touch us and comfort us, it teaches us how to be comforting, as our softer skills are shaped by the finer languages of music, images, dreams, reflections, and stories.

The Comfort of Sharing Art

As comforters, there are times when we run out of words to say or activities to propose, to help lift someone we care about out of their pain. At these times it can be especially beneficial to instead sit back with the person we wish to comfort and take refuge in the wide world of art and entertainment. Here are a few ways we can share works of art together.

JUST SITTING TOGETHER, SHARING ART AND ENTERTAINMENT

Simply sitting together and watching a beloved television show or movie or listening to a favorite piece of music with someone can be a highly comforting activity. Our companionship, as long as we are focused and honestly engaged in what they choose to share, is a simple and powerful way to connect heart to heart with someone in pain. I've heard beautiful stories of comforters spending their last weeks with loved ones at the end of their lives, sitting at their bedside, just sharing art and entertainment together on DVDs, TV, and radio.

One well-known and moving true story involves a ten-year-old girl, Colby Curtin, who was dying of cancer and dearly wanted to see the movie *Up* before her time ran out on earth. The producers of the Pixar movie, when contacted at the last minute, quickly provided a DVD of *Up* for her to view from her bed, as she was too weak to see it in a theater. The child enjoyed the video, smiled while it played, and died soon afterward. Though she could not open her eyes, and could only listen to the movie, her family was able to share this last wish coming true for her in the nick of time. Her mother was deeply touched by the story of *Up*, and was glad to share it with her daughter.

The images in the film of people going up into the sky with their balloons meant to her that Colby was going *up* to heaven, too.

RECORD A COMPILATION OF
YOUR LOVED ONE'S FAVORITE TUNES

Many people have told me in support groups their best comforts have been gifts made by loved ones of thoughtful compilations of their favorite music. A survivor of lung cancer who was often exhausted dearly enjoyed a CD her son burned for her, with uplifting songs he selected for her "that reminded him of my journey."

She continues, "I play it when I need a boost of energy. But mostly it's a great comfort to me, because I am still touched by how sweet he was to pick out my favorite singers and tunes. He remembered my old-timers like the Beatles, Stevie Nicks, and Randy Newman. I mean, the kid is only twenty, but he recorded music from *The Point*! I still can't believe how well he 'gets' me. It's like he knew my soul well enough to find the music that makes me smile."

SCRAPBOOKING TOGETHER

Scrapbooking has quickly become a popular pastime recently. It is fun to collect old photos, memorabilia, little souvenirs (letters), and other images, and make beautiful pages to tell the stories of our loved one's life. This can be done with our loved one or not, but it certainly is a gift that celebrates our loved one's journey.

READING AND RECITING POETRY, SONNETS, FAVORITE WRITINGS TOGETHER

One of my colleagues, Pam Blunt, an arts therapist (later profiled in this section) shared a story with me about her mother's last days of life that beautifully illustrates how art can bring people together:

"My mother loved the arts, and turned to them a great deal during the last year of her life. She found solace in poetry, literature, and music, a source of comfort and guidance for facing her grief after my father died, and her own illness and imminent death. During that time, she often spoke to me about how a poem or piece of music moved her and helped her understand some aspect of her experience. On one of the last nights we spent with her, my sister and I recorded her telling family stories from her life. We recited her favorite poems together, and we listened to Mozart. It was a sweet, intimate night spent with two women who are the most beloved to me in the world. Her last request to me was to recite Shakespeare's Sonnet 116, as she lay dying: 'Let me not to the marriage of true minds admit impediments. . . .' I hope it was as powerful and comforting for her as it was for me."

The Comfort of Creating Art
for Others and with Others

Equally as comforting to the comforter and the one being comforted as appreciating art is the whole experience of creating art. And we don't need to be artistically talented or gifted to enjoy the comfort of making things for or with our loved ones. The hands-on satisfaction of knitting, woodworking, photography, or home decorating are activities that naturally bring forth our unique creativity and innovation.

Channeling our human drive to express ourselves is comforting in itself. Singing (or ranting, as the case may be!) in the shower, ingeniously creating space in our closets, or doodling with our highlighters while our computer boots up—all of these simple creative acts can be satisfying outlets. In addition, our creations—be it our home-baked lasagna, herb sachets from our gardens, or a photo of ducks on a pond—can communicate our comfort in simple yet profound ways. Here are a few of the ways that we can use the creation of art to comfort others and ourselves:

• Grounds us, centers us

    Whether we are sewing pillows, playing a flute, carving wood, or acting in a play, we step into the present moment, out of our heads and egos, uniting ourselves with what we are creating. We touch the fabric, or reach for the notes of the flute. We shape the wood, or play with our voice, all requiring our full attention, our step-by-step process, our time. Even when we are overwhelmed with problems, immersing ourselves in these activities takes us into a healing, grounding space, perhaps into the creative force of life itself.

• Connects us, tethers us

When we share our stories, our crafts, our music, our photos, or even our cooking, people are drawn out of themselves in the act of enjoyment, or by their sheer curiosity. The gift we have created, no matter how simple, brings us together, in many different ways—over the dinner table, over the pages, over the blogs, over the radio, over the audience. Even if people don't always "get it" right away, most of them appreciate the action taken, the thoughtfulness, the effort.

• When we make things for others, we think "outside the box"

Something magical happens when our creation designed for another person has taken shape. It takes on a life of its own. It speaks to us, in its own way. Suddenly, our piece of art, what we thought was finished, morphs into something more, or something else. It asks for more from us. The pillows we made for our grandmother suddenly seem to look better on her bed than on her living room chairs, and before we know it, she asks us to make some more pillows for her chairs. She loves them so much, she wants your signature pillows in every room! We can make new pillows for her over the years for memorable occasions, such as her birthday, Christmas, her wedding anniversary, and many more opportunities. Pillow-making becomes a ritual of love, and we are challenged in a fun way to keep creating new designs. We step outside our box and become more creative than we think we really can be when people enjoy our comforting creations.

Art, any creation made for someone else, has a way of growing on them and on us, expanding beyond its original boundaries, asking us to stretch our imaginations. And when we reach with our minds and hearts to make art to comfort someone we care about, we are thinking outside the box of our own self-imposed limits and fears, and stepping into new areas and perspectives.

- Teaches us empathy, respect for others, comforting skills

Before I became a counselor, I taught drama and dance to children and teens for fifteen years, through the 1980s and into the mid-1990s. With the excitement of music, costume, props, and masks, the kids had a blast performing as Egyptians, Native Americans, Greek gods, Russians, runaway slaves, princesses, astronauts, explorers, cowboys, blind people, elderly people, homeless people.

Years later, I was delighted to hear from my students how the oral skills, movement skills, and teamwork skills were vital to their later success in communicating effectively as adults. But the most heartening news was that drama and dance had taught them the skills of empathy and respect for others, having walked in the shoes/sandals/ moccasins/boots of people in different cultures and backgrounds, as well as different eras. Becoming the people they were reading about or hearing about on TV had not only helped them understand other people better, it had made their world less scary and foreign. Acting and dance gave them the opportunity to portray through their characters the universal comforting traits of humor, kindness, wisdom, patience, empathy—timelessly comforting virtues in all cultures and classes.

* Helps us release emotions and heal

    Sometimes the best way to zap a bad mood is to pound a drum, strike the right chords on a piano, or get embroiled in your character's feisty dialogues in the novel you're writing. You could even dance till you drop. Certainly, these are all more productive channels for raw emotions than starting arguments, joining in nasty snarkiness and gossip on a blog, punching holes in our cubicles, or yelling at our pets.

    All the better to share the experience with someone who also needs a release—to paint a mural together or compose a short story together.

CHAPTER 7

The Healing Power
of Art in Action

Introducing Our Guides to
the Arts of Comforting

FROM MY EARLIER YEARS of teaching in the performing arts
through my later career as a counselor, I've met dozens
of inspirational colleagues and mentors applying the arts in
the fields of education, psychotherapy, nursing, and community development. Their passion, energy, and vision for what
they do year after year never ceases to amaze me. In the following pages I will introduce you to three of these master
comforters, a storyteller, a ceramic artist, and an expressive-
arts therapist.

Our guides to the arts of comforting are vibrant, resourceful people with a reverence for the spark of creativity that
dwells in all of us, and they use this energy to help people
heal. These aren't just talented artists and experts, well
known and vital to their communities; they are genuinely
comforting people at heart.

· ❧ ·

FINDING COMMON GROUND WITH STORIES
Les Schaffer

Storyteller

Cofounder and Director, Tell Tale Hearts Storytellers Theater, Richmond, Virginia

No matter what we've been through, or what we've lost, we always have a story left to tell.

Core Comforting Qualities: Wisdom and Humility
A natural-born storyteller, and cofounder of the Tell Tale Hearts Storytellers Theater in Richmond, Les Schaffer takes his audiences through the twists and turns of his adventures and misadventures with humor, intrigue, and tenderness. Les travels throughout Virginia with his troupe, performing for a wide range of audiences at festivals, retreat centers, addiction treatment programs, nursing homes, schools, colleges, community centers, and libraries, and everywhere he goes his audiences hoot with laughter. Les always lives up to his signature quote, "All my stories are true, even the ones I make up."

Les derives his wisdom and passion for storytelling from his long, rich career as a family and children's counselor. For more than twenty years in a community mental health center, Les used storytelling as a therapeutic tool to resolve family conflict. Les encouraged children and parents to pick their favorite characters with whom they most identified and to act as if they were that character being confronted with a situation or situations similar to that of their own. Using this creative play therapy, Les's clients were able to explore the consequences of their character's choices and behaviors and, ultimately, search for solutions to their real-life problems.

Les was so convinced and inspired by the healing power of storytelling that he cofounded the Tell Tale Hearts Storytellers Theater in 1999. Drawing on his extensive experience utilizing storytelling within a therapeutic environment, Les now carefully chooses and adapts the best stories to meet the specialized needs of his audience. He improvises easily with them, inviting them to participate out loud, as he flexes his lines and gestures to respond to their impromptu requests. More than a performer and theater director, Les facilitates healing events, drawing forth the creativity, courage, and compassion of his audiences as they observe and join in his stories.

I'VE SAT DOWN WITH LES many times over the past few years to talk about the healing power of storytelling, and about how being a storyteller has helped him heal from his own battle with prostate cancer.

According to Les, we can derive a great deal of comfort from telling our stories about the most difficult and challenging aspects of our lives. This is because when we tell a story about a painful experience it forces us to reach for some kind of narrative, to offer a sequence of events—beginning, middle, and end. We might stutter, or repeat ourselves, grasp awkwardly for the right words, meander, and pause, but good listeners, good comforters, don't mind that at all. They follow us quietly as we find the words to describe how our journey unfolded and, ultimately, what meaning we take from it by way of a conclusion. And suddenly, our story told—our pain shared—some of the weight of the world is lifted off our shoulders.

Les says, "Every day I witness the ways stories connect us. Even with just a few sentences, storytelling is an antidote to isolation. I've seen the most devastated people find connection and a sense of belonging by joining with others to tell their stories."

Les shares his own account of the power of storytelling in facing his diagnosis of moderately advanced prostate cancer in 2005. "I was scared and felt terribly isolated. Nothing comforted me until I was able to hear another older man tell me his cancer survival story. I could have searched the Internet for advice, seen a hundred doctors, gotten the best treatment in the world, but having a regular guy tell me his story of how he faced his illness was the most comforting thing I encountered."

Les marveled at how this ordinary man's story about battling cancer changed his life.

"The chord he struck in me was that it was okay to be scared, downright petrified—scared to the point of paralysis. This guy's fear totally shut him down. In agonizing detail, he told me how it took him all day to get up the guts to phone the doctor for an appointment, after not sleeping the night before. Just hearing about these minute-by-minute and day-to-day dilemmas of dealing with gripping fear unlocked me from feeling so isolated and ashamed of my own fear. Facing cancer as a man, afraid of my own cowardice as much as the cancer itself, I was so relieved to find how much I had in common with another man I admired. His story gave me common ground to stand on for braving this strange new world of life-threatening illness."

Les outlines this man's story to demonstrate four ways in which stories comfort us:

1. Stories connect us. After the frightening news of having cancer, an older man telling me about how he first reacted to his diagnosis reassured me I was not alone in feeling so afraid. Stories alleviate our isolation.

2. Stories teach us survival skills, especially how to face adversity. When I talked with this cancer survivor about how he handled his chemo sessions, I was better informed and more prepared to face my treatment. Stories teach survival skills on many levels, socially, financially, physically, spiritually, morally.

3. Stories inspire us. This kind man shared his spiritual journey with me, and how facing his own mortality made him more compassionate and grateful for his life. Stories spark what moves and motivates us.

4. Stories reveal and clarify issues for us. When I heard this man describe how he procrastinated making phone calls for his medical appointments, it opened my eyes to what fear was doing to me. This alerted me to how much more support I needed to get for myself. Whenever we tell a story, we weave together the fragments and pieces of our lives into patterns, themes, directions. Stories give our experiences structure, meaning, and closure, even those experiences that had once seemed insignificant or obstructive. More than just venting, we can usually recognize a message in our narrative that rings true for us. The message of a story will keep us going. And better still, we can share the wisdom of our stories with others.

Les wonders how he would have fared in his recovery from cancer without Tell Tale Hearts and all that his experiences with his troupe and his audiences have taught him. "I bet that doing what I love doing, and loving the people I love has kept me going this strong for so long."

Les's Suggestions for Families or Other Groups to Inspire Storytelling

One evening, while enjoying a Mediterranean meal with hummus, tapas, falafel, and colorful veggies spread across our table, Les and I brainstormed on the ways that families could use storytelling to create simple, comforting moments together.

- Create movie theme nights

    Most people need props, "conversation pieces," or ice-breakers before the stories they might like to share start percolating. Movies, TV shows, games, sports, party food, music, holiday cooking, and craft activities are highly popular ways to get people in the mood for telling stories about their lives. Once the group has enjoyed the entertainment, elect a "moderator" to then steer the conversation toward storytelling. Following are some ideas for how this might be done using television show and movies:

    Star Trek episodes can serve as a launching point for stories about adventures in strange new worlds—how we navigated environments or situations that were new to us.

    Old classics with Buster Keaton, Charlie Chaplin, Laurel and Hardy, and the Three Stooges might inspire us to talk about the humor in painful experiences.

    Diva nights with movies celebrating strong women will naturally inspire groups of women to talk about difficult moments in their lives when they discovered that they were much stronger than they thought. Superhero movies like *Spider-Man* or *Batman* can have a similar effect on young boys in terms of bringing forth stories of discovering untapped "special powers."

- Read stories to children.

    Stories teach children how to deal with adversity in all areas of life. Kids are comforted when another kid or animal protagonist in a story figures out how to resolve a big problem.

In "Hansel and Gretel," the children learn the rewards of resourcefulness in leaving bread crumbs along their path.

In *Alexander and the Terrible, Horrible, No Good, Very Bad Day*, we learn the world doesn't fall apart when things are going badly.

In "The Three Little Pigs," we learn how the pigs outsmart the big bad wolf. We can solve problems, even at scary times, with a bit of ingenuity and drive.

In "The Frog Prince," we learn not to base decisions on appearances, or we might miss a wonderful surprise.

- Get together to listen to elder family members tell their stories of how they survived. *For example,* when we listen to our grandparents tell us how they survived during the Depression of the 1930s, we might learn ways to cope with our struggling economy in 2009.

  Do special things at dinnertime like lighting a candle to signal that tonight you will linger longer at the table and honor your time together more. At the end of a long day, a family or group dinner can be a wonderful way to connect and tell stories about our days or our lives in general.

- Create special celebrations. Why wait for official holidays to sit down and reconnect with your loved ones? Instead, create occasions to celebrate accomplishments (getting A's on a report card or passing a tough exam; Mom's new look with a bold haircut; a friend's graduation). Bake cookies, make garlands, make banners, blow up balloons, hand out wacky little party favors or souvenirs, read riddles out loud. Create special new spaces in which you can exchange stories about proud moments in your lives.

• Start a book club or a discussion group *(salon).*

Is there anything better than a good book to elicit stories from each other in a group? After general discussion of the given book, make time for the group to tell stories connected to the themes the book introduced.

· ❦ ·

GRACIOUSNESS UNDER PRESSURE

Amy Handy
Artist, Writer, Editor
Owner, Clay Play, Yarmouth, Maine

People are so afraid of doing things wrong when they try something new. I love telling people "There is no wrong way to do this" when they make pottery with us. Being gracious is essential for people to feel safe here.

Core Comforting Qualities: Warmth and Graciousness
What's comforting on a restless Saturday afternoon in snowy Yarmouth, Maine, when the kids are running high cabin fevers and you've run out of things to do? Head to Clay Play, where

owner Amy Handy beckons people to explore their own curiosity and wonder while their clay creations take shape.

One cold December day I visited Clay Play and found Amy rotating between the many tables, periodically running to the back of the store to grab fresh supplies or to check on the kiln. Radiating graciousness under pressure, she smiles the whole time, chatting easily with staff and customers.

I listen to a delightful cacophony of voices across the busy tables, as people of all ages converse while working on their pieces. Grown-ups catch up on who's doing what in their lives. An eight-year-old boy talks excitedly about the gift he is making. "This is for my Grandma's birthday. She loves apples, so I'm painting bright red apples all over this cup." Family members visiting from out of town catch up with their host relatives as they all paint mugs together. Children share stories about favorite characters from books, movies, and TV, as the grown-ups listen and comment. Wizards, fairies, cartoon characters are painted on plates and trays. Elders share recollections about favorite objects and keepsakes, triggered by the pieces they are creating.

I met Amy at a "newcomers club" when I first moved to Maine ten years ago. Amy quickly put me at ease by introducing me to the smiling women sitting next to her, as well as her daughter, Veronica, a toddler who was enjoying the chatter and attention around her. Over the years, she invited me to speak for the club's monthly events, and after the event we'd relax over a late dinner, absorbed in fascinating conversations about the healing power of art.

Amy, her husband, and her older daughter, Julia, moved from New York to Maine just a few years before I arrived. We both loved Yarmouth and the greater Portland area, finding plenty of artistic and enterprising people in small, vibrant communities along the coast.

For more than twenty years, Amy has been an editor of art, craft, and design books, and has worked with Amazon.com and Abbeville Press. She is the author of several books, including *American Castles: A Pictorial History*. Before becoming a book editor, she was a production manager for the costume house Eaves-Brooks in New York City. In addition to her editing work, she has designed and produced costumes for Ogunquit Playhouse and served as props coordinator for the Portland Stage Company in Maine.

Amy goes with the flow better than anyone I've ever met. Extremely imaginative and resourceful, she can improvise with anything tossed her way: too many customers, too few customers, pushy customers, crying toddlers, paint spills across the floor, pottery dropped on the floor, fighting siblings, lost wallets, tired and complaining moms. If necessity is the mother of invention, then, for Amy, necessity is the mother of creative genius.

Amy's passion and joy bursts forth when she speaks about the comfort of making crafts. According to Amy, "Making things with our hands is comforting—*period*. It's truly comforting to feel different textures and shape things with our hands, whether we're quilting, sewing, weaving baskets, decorating wreaths, baking, playing with clay, planting seeds, scrapbooking, or knitting."

Amy has been particularly impressed with how teenagers interact with one another while doing hands-on art activities—when they can get away from texting for a while! "I love watching how relaxed and friendly teenagers can be with each other when they are painting pottery at a table together. Girls seem to enjoy making gifts for each other, particularly when they are first getting to know each other. This helps develop their relationships and push past the peer pressure to fit in."

It is Amy's hope that through her work at Clay Play she can help to restore a highly comforting time in our past when the creation of crafts grounded and connected us.

"People are hungry for hands-on activities, especially group activities, many of which have been lost in our contemporary society. But these lost arts are being restored. As an editor of craft books for the past twenty years, I've observed that user-friendly craft books, for practical and decorative uses, as well as good old-fashioned home economics, are making a comeback, especially as our world economy weakens. People with less money to spend are rediscovering the comfort and practical uses of crafts. With some of our repeat customers at Clay Play, I've often heard people remark that making pottery inspired them to do more crafts at home, and to be creative in finding new ways to use their old stuff. It heartens me to learn how people have pulled their old curtains out of boxes and cleverly hung them up again, made new pillows to brighten up their living room sofas, or mended old quilts to hang on hallway walls. Creating fresh new uses for old things is one of life's greatest comforts."

Amy's Comforting Practices at Clay Play

Amy is a master at calmly reassuring people that it's okay for them to experiment with clay. She explains how she provides comfort to help first-time artists get past their fears and awkwardness:

"First, I say to my guests, There is no wrong way to do this.

"Accommodating them is the key to their success. I adapt the project to the customer's skill level and background. I show them samples that fit their skill level, and offer stamps, stencils, and idea files full of pictures. I watch how they react to the samples, and tune in to what might be obstacles for them. I help them think of ways to get around obstacles and show them materials that excite and inspire them.

"Next, I ask them questions to help them make choices and decisions about their piece.

"I ask if they are making something for someone else or themselves. If they are making the piece for someone else, I find out more about the person they are making it for, as this often gets them motivated and more interested in their project. I ask gentle questions to help guide their process: 'Do you want to make something practical or more decorative?' 'Is this just for fun?' 'Is this going in your kitchen, or what room in your home?' 'What colors are your favorite?'

"Because people can be intimidated by staring at a blank piece of paper or a blank piece of pottery, I offer easy tools such as stencils or rubber stamps, so no one needs to create 'from scratch.' People are often more comfortable using images and designs they can play with, rather than making their own drawings to paint.

"As they progress to the final phases of their piece, I share in their joy and surprise as they watch their work take shape. Talking about the uses for the piece or where it will be displayed brings out smiles and fresh ideas. It's usually quite evident, by the way people hold the finished product in their hands, that they are truly comforted by their creation."

Amy's Comforting Art-Making Activities for Families

• Go to a pottery studio and paint your own ceramic art.

Amy encourages families to discover local paint-your-own pottery studios (like Clay Play) in their own communities. Over the past decade or so, studios of this type have sprung up throughout America, providing a very affordable and fun creative activity (for nationwide listings, visit www.paintyourownpottery.net).

• Make a family tree or a family collage of your relatives and ancestors.

Research family genealogy. Use a computer program to assemble a family tree, or draw one out on a big sheet of paper. Photocopy or scan old family photos and pictures of ancestors to incorporate into the tree.

• Make and decorate cookies.

Since you'll be eating your work and not leaving any permanent record, some people may be less afraid to be creative.

• Make gifts for any occasion. Some easy and inexpensive things:

A box of handmade cards (stamped, sponged, or painted).
A framed page of collaged images or photos with a special message for someone.
Beading—for simple bracelets, necklaces, ornaments, and other decorative art.

• Make decorations for any occasion. It's always comforting to make thoughtful decorations, not just for holidays, but also to simply add a personal touch to our surroundings. Textures, favorite colors, touches of humor, keepsakes, and little pockets of beauty can soften the edges of our rooms, corners, and furniture.

Decorate windows, walls, large potted plants, or shelves with things such as a string of tiny lights, garlands, ribbons, silk or dried flowers, scarves, ornaments, fabrics, quilts and throws, wreaths, stones, baskets, driftwood.

Make fun mobiles to hang from the ceiling, such as stars, comets, suns, angels, rainbows, origami pieces, flying fairies, flying birds, flying planes . . . flying anything.

Check clearance sections of craft stores and stock up on odds and ends that can be incorporated into other projects. For example, red Christmas items can be turned into Valentine's Day decor.

- Make little fairy houses.

Get a group of children together outdoors to make a little village of fairy houses, using bits of natural objects (pebbles, shells, twigs, feathers, moss, dried flowers, or leaves glued to cardboard) for a magical time together. These houses can later be brought indoors and saved on a special shelf or viewing place.

Veronica's Tips

Amy's creative daughter, Veronica (age twelve), suggests these comforting art activities, using a wall in a bedroom, kitchen, or hallway:

- Make a section of your wall into a display area for sticky notes, and then collect fun messages from your friends or relatives when they come to visit you. Or use a large bulletin board to tack on their friendly messages, photos, and cards.
- Use chalkboard paint or magnetic paint to turn a section of your wall into a special viewing spot. You can put magnetic

letters and images on the magnetic paint, and draw with colored chalk on the chalkboard paint.

- Make maps on poster board of places where you would like to go, or of fantasy places, and hang them on your wall.
- Make welcome signs for your guests on posters or banners. It's fun to use different languages for signs too.
- And, of course, refrigerators are perfect places for magnetic letters, images and pictures, funny comics, and photos.

Veronica also suggests using tracing paper to copy images and shapes, and also stencils for designs to paint decorations for cards, collages, boxes, and pottery.

• ❧ •

SHINING A LIGHT ON ONE ANOTHER
Pamela Blunt, LCSW
Expressive Arts Therapist, Artist, Social Worker
Bisbee, Arizona

We need to be seen one another. We can't recognize ourselves all by ourselves.

Core Comforting Qualities: Validation and Hopefulness
Pamela Blunt has a lovely voice, warm and resonant with soft, low tones. I could just sit back, close my eyes, and listen to her talk about anything. I can understand why her clients keep coming back. She simply sounds comforting.

Pam's generous spirit makes her the perfect companion

for creative acts of all kinds, be it singing out loud or drawing a picture. Pam works a great deal with elderly people,
many of whom have never made art before, and she has a gift
for making them feel safe to explore their creative selves for
the first time in their lives.

I have worked with Pam as a colleague, and have first-
hand experience with her co-creative spirit. She possesses
an uncanny ability to shine a light on our creative abilities,
often hidden inside us and unrecognized. She sees strengths
we might not have seen in ourselves, spots a talent or a gift
we might have undermined or overlooked. She heartens us
to take our creative abilities seriously, whether we choose
to develop them for our own personal growth or cultivate
them professionally. To Pam, we are all creative at heart, but
we usually do not recognize our creativity all by ourselves
in a vacuum. Says Pam, "Without being witnessed by others, we don't see our potential, our talents, our callings."
Pam laments how the excesses of rugged individualism in
our culture have perpetuated myths about "finding ourselves" all by ourselves, just by looking within. "But we are
relational beings and our talents and gifts usually show up
when we are interacting in some way with others, when we
get ourselves out of the way to express something important
to others."

Pam once shined a light on me when I was confused and
discouraged in my mid-twenties, juggling between finishing
my BFA in theater, teaching drama and dance, and doing *many*
part-time jobs to support myself as an artist and arts teacher.

I had little encouragement for all the energy I was putting into trying to be an artist while keeping a roof over my head.

I first met Pam in 1980 in our hometown of Richmond, Virginia, in a hip little vegetarian restaurant called the Grace Place. I was her waitress, and she was a friend of a friend. She kindly overlooked how bad a waitress I was, as I continued to forget her side order of falafel with each chatty visit I made to her table, but we hit it off quite well. By the time her falafel was finally delivered, we found ourselves in the midst of a passionate discussion about *The Power of Myth* by Joseph Campbell and the meanings of our dreams.

Pam frequented the Grace Place, and after my shifts, we often shared our journals of our dreams and visions. She was well ahead of her time in exploring the connections between dance, myth, anthropology, and body work, while finishing her bachelor's degree in anthropology at the University of Arizona and studying with healers and dancers. She captivated me with her thoughts on our creative processes, and how our body's wisdom honestly tells us what our souls are calling us to. She indeed validated my inner wisdom about myself, inspiring my early calling as an artist.

After settling permanently in Arizona, Pam worked as a massage therapist in private practice and at Canyon Ranch for ten years, then went for her graduate degree in social work. Initially she worked with children under the care of Child Protective Services, her natural passion for the arts leading her to integrate music, painting, movement, and drama into her work with them. She later shared these same expressive activities in a rural home-based hospice with adults who were dying and their loved ones.

In 2000, Pam began a five-year postgraduate course of study in intermodal expressive arts therapies at the International School for Interdisciplinary Studies in Tucson, Arizona, and later at the European Graduate School in Saas Fee, Switzerland. Currently Pam works with elders with disabilities, bringing arts therapies to their homes and to nursing homes. She also meets clients for sessions in her spacious art studio in Bisbee, Arizona, where she creates her own paintings and ceramics.

She and her husband, Monte Surratt, an artist on the faculty of Cochise College, are highly involved with two artist cooperatives in Bisbee, collaborating with other artists on events throughout the year.

To my surprise and delight, when Pam and I sit down to discuss the healing power of art, she'd rather explore the questions I ask her by asking *me* questions, engaging me in a fluid dialogue. It's no surprise, as an expressive arts therapist, that she brings out the playful side of me while sharing her own joy along the way. Quite frankly, she is the easiest brain I have ever picked, bursting with great tips for both professional and personal applications of comfort.

What strikes me is Pam's reverence for the power of expression, artistic or otherwise, our vital, human need to create and give life to what arrives through our imagination; to shape it with sound, movement, words, story, and/or imagery.

"There are no 'uncreative' people. Everyone has a well-spring of experiences, longings, fantasies, stories, ways of moving, tones of voice, which can be shared, played with, enlarged upon. What I find comforting about facilitating these experiences with people is how natural and simple it is. There is joy in the surprises that happen when we are immersed in an activity that we are really making up as we go along. I love witnessing people discovering their creative power. I can see the wonderment and delight on their faces at their very spontaneous and unique creations. Often an experience can be sacred, deep, and hilarious all at the same time. Many times people return to tell me that they were inspired to continue to create on their own, or with friends and family, based on something they created during a session."

Pam says she never tires of being midwife to the imaginations of her clients, as she is often awed by what people create spontaneously with the simplest of tools: our hands, feet, voices, words, and most of all, our hearts. She might coax the dancer out of a woman with advanced multiple sclerosis, doing "hand dances" to the music of her favorite CD. She might laugh with an elder as he records his life story on a tape recorder. With someone else, it may be an original song that emerges, created out of a poem, in turn created out of the simple spoken words from a session. Or she might assist a family in creating an impromptu shrine for a loved one out of materials gathered in the desert around their home or from their kitchen drawers. All these activities require heartfelt interaction, spontaneity, and tender attention, fostered by Pam's presence. But she laments how people censor themselves, and as a therapist she tries to free people from their inner critics.

"Most of us suffer from the societal habit of having to explain things all the time, to justify things we create for others and to ourselves, instead of experiencing an activity honestly and deeply. People can be so hard on themselves, censoring themselves from the full experience of making art, fearing they are not qualified to be artistic. This is so sad. I've worked with people late in their lives in their sixties, seventies, and eighties, who had never allowed themselves to leisurely and joyously do the artistic things they had always wanted to do."

She deeply believes we yearn to be witnessed and heard, and, most of all, moved. When we are moved, our creative response can surprise us, flowing beyond what we first had in mind—beckoning more from us. This yearning to be moved and to express what is in our hearts is the fiery source of our soul.

Pam's Tips for Helping People Find Healing Through Art

- First and foremost, offering my full attention.

    This requires a slowed-down pace, and being comfortable with stillness and silence.

Asking simple, open-ended questions, not to probe, not to examine, but just to gently explore. I might simply ask, "What's going on for you this week?" I often recapitulate what they have said, to show I am following them, and caring about what they are saying.

- Being willing to play.

    It's important to have a willingness to be involved in the art-making, too, to play together, not just to observe. I lead the activity just enough for someone to feel safe, but hang back enough for them to take a risk—it's a responsive dance based on paying attention. But it's really not that different from the way that children engage in dramatic play—making offers, going with what the other child makes up.

- Listening closely, and tuning in to their body language. I notice how people warm up or cool down about the topics they bring up, what energizes them or drains them. What makes them smile or squirm or grimace. I offer feedback. It's important to know what energizes us and what drains us—gives us conscious choices to make that can improve the daily quality of our lives. Just having choices about formerly unquestioned behaviors can be comforting.

- Bringing them into awareness of the present moment through the senses. I often ask them to close their eyes and tell me what their senses are telling them, what they are perceiving in their surroundings and in their bodies. They might say, "I hear birds singing outside . . . I feel my lower back is a little tight . . . I smell a nice scent of pine in the air . . . I notice my breathing." While they are relating this stream of consciousness, this awareness of their senses, I am writing down what they say. Later, I share with them what they said, and we might put this into a poem, or into a dance, or into a painting. Just allowing them to pay attention to the moment can reveal how rich our world around us and inside of us really is. By just being present in this way, people are comforted, no matter how limited their physical condition. Children love to do this exercise as well.

Paradoxically, of course, this experiment always brings people into a deeper sense of connection with other people and with the earth. I remember a woman who was blind and very depressed due to advanced diabetes. She was moved to tears when she realized that for a long time, she had not taken the time to listen to the many sounds in her environment, to touch the many textures. She said she felt the whole world was open to her again through this simple exercise. Another client severely crippled by rheumatoid arthritis now regularly writes poetry based on this exercise. The wonderful thing is that no matter how many times we engage in this awareness focus, it is always different and new.

Pam's Comforting Suggestions for Families
- Touch

Even if no one is trained in massage or Healing Touch, just placing our hands gently but fully in contact over the ankles, knees, wrists can be very warming and relaxing. Foot baths and foot rubs using aromatherapy oils or mineral salts are delicious. Putting on lotion and rubbing it in is soothing, especially after a foot bath. Encourage the ones we are comforting to take long, full breaths.

- Playing music that they find comforting

    It's a thoughtful and comforting thing to put on music someone especially enjoys (even if we don't like it that much). When we know it comforts our loved one in distress, it feels good to show we are thinking of them by saying, "I put on some music just for you this evening."

- Playing board games and card games and doing puzzles

    Games are convenient, comforting, and reliable ways to gather family members and/or friends together. Games provide structure and routine for families going through transition, crisis, or loss, and can be opportunities for people to come together in undemanding, lighthearted havens of good, old-fashioned fun.

    Some all-time favorites (some come in junior versions) for most child and adult players (many are available online now):

Monopoly
Pictionary
Checkers
Clue

Sorry

Guess Who?

Yahtzee

Scrabble

Twister

Battleship

Cranium

Chutes and Ladders

- Watch game shows on TV like *Jeopardy!* or *Wheel of Fortune.*
- Play old-time favorite games such as Tag, Hide-and-Seek, Red Rover, Frozen Statues, Hot and Cold, Simon Says. On a rainy day, it can be really fun to play Hide-and-Seek throughout the house with friends and neighbors.

Pam's Activities for Bereaved Families

- Create a shrine.

A shrine could be arranged on a small table, a chest, a bookshelf, or in a quiet corner or nook. Some people create a collection of textures, pictures, and small objects and frame this gathering of things as a picture to hang on the wall.

We can include all of our senses in how we choose objects in honor of our loved ones for our shrine.

Visual: We can place pictures, photos, small objects, memorabilia, art, sculpture.

Sound: Place bells, music boxes, or musical cards.

Touch: Use textures, fabrics, nature objects (conch shells, stones, feathers, pine cones, driftwood).

Smell: Douse perfumes on fabrics, use aromatherapy oils or candles.

• Make a memory box or container.

This is also a kind of shrine, but it is portable and can be put away if needed.

Inside and outside the box, decorate it with paints or collage to express your thoughts, feelings, and memories about the deceased. Put special things inside the box, small keepsakes and memorabilia. One client enjoyed this so much that she ended up creating a large playful, movable sculpture with her children in their yard, as if the yard was their "box." Truly, "thinking outside the box"!

• Create a ritual.

Using favorite songs, poems, prayers, blessings, or sayings of our loved one, it can be as simple or as elaborate as we want to express. Decide as a family when and how often a ritual will be practiced. Lighting a candle and just saying out loud the words we have written in memory of our loved one is very healing. Often it helps to include each family member participating in the ritual to be responsible for a certain task. One person can light the candle and say an opening statement; the next person can read a prayer; then someone tells a short story or sings a song. Children and teens certainly benefit from participating.

- Make a memory wreath or decorate a memory tree.

  To commemorate our loved ones, little pictures, ornaments, objects, origami shapes, and nature pieces can be
  placed on wreaths or small trees (often made with silk
  flowers, dried flowers, plastic, or papier-mâché). I once saw
  a beautiful white little plastic tree decorated with blue and
  gold origami (folded paper) shapes of Pegasus horses, stars,
  suns, and moons, in honor of a person who loved horses.

- Make a scrapbook.

  Children and family members can write and draw
  around the photos of their loved one. Some children like to
  create a "cartoon" or "graphic" journal of memories.

PART FOUR

The Nature of
Comforting

What Animals and
the Earth Teach Us

CHAPTER 8

Comfort from the Heart of Nature

Chickadees

ONE JUNE MORNING, as I sat happily on a warm, mossy rock in Wolfe's Neck Woods on the Casco Bay, a pair of chickadees swirled around me. One of them, a male, landed at the end of a branch in a spindly birch tree, right over my head. He seemed quite intrigued, as he fixed his gaze upon me, head tilted just so. I sat still, entranced by his intense, charming gaze. Suddenly, as if I were someone he knew well and trusted, he hopped onto my head. Amazed, I sat still, just feeling his warm little body, softly breathing and seeming in no hurry to leave. And then quietly he lowered his beak and lightly tapped me on my forehead—a tiny kiss. Afterward, he flew off, landing back on the branch above me. Smitten, I beamed a smile back at him as he continued to watch me. Everything in my world stopped as we lingered sweetly, staring into each other's eyes, our souls joining together. In just a few minutes, this tiny bird made sacred all that I loved in creation.

Ever since my chickadee initiation, I am especially attuned to their calls outside my window, even when I am fretting over bills, flu pandemics, the Taliban in Pakistan, or how loudly my neighbors like to play their music. They never cease to pull me out of my human drama du jour, drawing my racing imagination into their trees, hilltops, and skies.

I am convinced the earth can give us great solace, wisdom, and hope, especially when our human-to-human experiences disappoint us or leave us lonely. After all, in nature, we are never really alone—the web of life, with all of its mysteries, surrounds and supports us. As comforters, one of the most powerful things we can do to help someone in pain is to bring them back to this great, unending source of peace. And as humans in need of comforting ourselves, it is important to remember that sometimes the greatest "medicine" is a quiet walk in the woods.

Beholding

I will never forget the pure connection I felt to that chickadee as he sat on that branch beholding me. The memory serves as a constant reminder that the way in which we behold someone in distress is as important as any comforting words we might say to them.

Over the years, I have watched comforting people in the

act of beholding the ones they are tending to. There is a certain genuine, soft look in their eyes. According to the *Oxford Dictionary*, the Old English origin of *behold* is *bi* (thoroughly) *halden* (hold), to "thoroughly hold." Stretching further, the definition of *thoroughly*: "performed with great care" and "regarded in every detail."

Don't we all hunger to be beheld in this way? Sometimes more than being heard, or even held, what we need is to *be beheld* in a dignified, respectful, yet warm and welcoming way. We crave recognition and acceptance, one soul to another, an "unconditional positive regard," as in Carl Rogers's person-centered counseling approach. The Sanskrit greeting *namaste* says it all: "The light in me recognizes the light in you."

For seventeen years my cat, Ivan, beheld me sweetly each day in his morning ritual of rolling on his back and staring at me with his gaga eyes as if I were his diva. Moments of comfort I remember best involve someone gazing upon me with love or tenderness or with kindness or respect. Just the look on these people's or animals' faces—some of whom had only briefly stepped into my life, like my chickadee, or a giggling toddler who once sat across the aisle from me on a train—linger in my memory as eternal sources of comfort.

Animals and nature remind us that we shortchange ourselves and those around us if we miss experiencing the great comfort of being both on and *of* this earth. They remind us that it is only when we observe thoroughly and listen deeply that we are truly "there" for ourselves and others.

Comforting Suggestions for Families or Other Groups
to Connect with Animals and Nature

We can give back to our communities by volunteering with animals and nature as rewarding and meaningful work. Here are a few ideas:

- Pet therapy programs
- Humane societies
- Recycling projects
- Environmental projects—planting trees, cleaning up trails
- Nature centers, parks
- Going bird-watching or hiking on trails together
- Starting a garden in a private or community space or growing plants indoors
- Playing with our pets

Introducing Our Guides
to the Nature of Comforting

I am fortunate to know many healers who learned the nonverbal languages of comforting from the natural world around them. They have studied, partnered with, and applied this life-affirming wisdom with many groups of people, including those who are grieving, distressed, or chronically ill.

Don and Brenda Weeks, a gentle and compassionate

married couple, work with their therapy dogs, going to hospitals, nursing homes, and hospices. They present to us what
they have learned from dogs about reaching out to people
in distress who are often isolated, withdrawn, and afraid in
their pain. Nancy Coyne, M.D., is a warm and wise psychiatrist working with horses as healers for trauma survivors,
including those with severe PTSD, such as veterans of the
Iraq War, victims of violent crime, and survivors of domestic
abuse. Laura Hare has developed innovative and successful
programs that show children how to be responsible caregivers
and team players by directly caring for animals.

Finally, Jen Deraspe, a wilderness retreat director and
mindfulness instructor, shows us how to find stillness and
quietude so we can behold the comfort of the earth—and the
peace within ourselves.

· ❦ ·

DOG WISDOM: EVERYONE DESERVES COMFORTING
Don and Brenda Weeks
Providers of the Therapy Dog Program at
Central Maine Medical Center
Owners, Directors, and Trainers, Shangri-La Kennel,
Auburn, Maine

*For people in distress during unpredictable times, dogs can be a
predictable comfort. Dogs allow us the freedom to let our own
walls down, so we can be present with each other.*

Core Comforting Qualities: Acceptance and Compassion

Don and Brenda Weeks smile modestly as I ask them what dogs teach us about comforting. They have poured me an icy Coke and seated me at a table in their huge country kitchen with two of their dogs, Savannah, a black Lab, and Onyx, a flat-coated retriever, lying politely beside my feet. Wearing sandals, I can feel Onyx's wagging tail gently swooshing across my feet and shins, which is fine with me. The tail becomes a kind of barometer, responding to the level of excitement or intensity of our conversation. When we laugh, I feel her tail knocking against my feet, and when we settle back down, her tail slows back to its original leisurely pace.

I giggle as Onyx suddenly begins to lightly lick my hand. Don and Brenda chuckle softly at their dog's uncanny ability to sense exactly what I need at this moment, relieving some of my shyness and pre-interview tension. Already, one thing is clear about what dogs can teach us about comforting— they remind us not to take ourselves so seriously.

Married for twenty-six years, Don and Brenda have quietly and humbly devoted themselves to running a kennel, training therapy dogs and volunteers, and collaborating with medical staff all over central Maine. Don and Brenda met while studying to be certified guide dog instructors at the Guiding Eyes School for the Blind in Yorktown Heights, New York, in the early 1980s. Earlier, they had both gone to the same school at Holliston Junior College in Massachusetts for their kennel management certificate. Since 1993, they have been visiting patients in local nursing homes and

Central Maine Medical Center with several of their therapy dogs.

Brenda, who has coped with multiple sclerosis for sixteen years, uses a power chair and a vent but functions beautifully with the dogs when she goes on visits to nursing homes and hospices.

Don and Brenda emphasize how important it is to sit back and let the dogs have the spotlight when they're doing a therapy visit at a hospital. They gently guide the dogs so patients can focus their full attention on them. I soon learn what makes pet therapy professionals so good at what they do—they keep out of the way and stay in the background yet somehow direct their dogs remotely, invisibly. This is quite an art in itself.

Brenda has a sweet, almost angelic face, and she positively beams when she talks about the work the dogs do. "When people don't know what to say, a dog is someone everyone can relate to—can touch, can talk about, like a conversation piece. Everyone can connect with the dog in some way, to be playful and relax a little. The therapy dog changes the mood and the whole energy of the patient's room. The patient, family members, and hospital staff will often laugh, slow down a little, and connect with each other in a way they hadn't before."

Don adds, smiling and nodding, "Dogs pull us out of our shells. People start to tell stories, even long stories, especially about dogs they've had, or other pet stories. Everyone has some kind of an animal story, and we often feel safer telling animal stories than other personal stories. The animal stories ultimately lead them on to relating personal stories about themselves, their fears, their worries, and what might lie ahead for them. We're always humbled that they feel comfortable enough with us to share tales they haven't told others before."

"And these stories can be funny, too, a great icebreaker," Brenda joins in. "A good dog story can unify everyone, bring a family or a group of friends together with memories of good times—summer vacations, or trips, or birthday parties or weddings. It's interesting how many of these stories are about dogs in group events, not just private moments. Dog stories can take a family down memory lane together, and they certainly help the patient at the hospital or hospice find enjoyable things to talk about, connect with."

I was curious what Don and Brenda, as comforters, were learning personally from dogs.

Don turns his answer over in his mind for a few moments and then says, "I have been working toward becoming a chaplain at Central Maine Medical Center's training program, and have also been volunteering as a Eucharist minister, bringing communion to patients at a hospice house and nursing homes. Working with our dog Christophe and meeting patients has convinced me that I need to develop more unconditional love and acceptance for people. I still struggle with some judgmental qualities in myself, and I know this interferes with my comforting abilities as a chaplain. Christophe shows me how being present and attuned to the patients' needs can pull me out of my rush to judgment and cynicism about human nature."

He tells a moving story about a man who struggled with alcoholism most of his life, lying alone in a hospital, dying of cirrhosis. "No one came to visit this man in his last days of life, as he had alienated everyone in his family, his ex-wife, his kids, and his friends. Aside from the medical staff, Christophe and I came to visit him every day. This patient understood and accepted why no one came to see him. He told me how he thought only a dog would be able to love him unconditionally, after all the trouble he had caused others in his life. He invited Christophe to jump up on his bed and lie down beside him. Christophe allowed this man to hold and caress him, and he returned his affection. He told me he had missed his own dog from an earlier time in his life, and thanked us with tears for having this opportunity to hold a dog once more at the end of his life."

Don pauses, gently noticing how moved Brenda and I are, as my eyes moisten a little with tears, then he tenderly continues, "I know this is really sad, but just imagine how *much* Christophe gave this man. It wasn't just the love, it was the freedom of being completely accepted, just as you are, all the good, the bad, *everything* . . . so you might find some peace at the end of your life. That is what I want to give people as a chaplain when they are in pain, emotionally or physically. I'll never be able to do this as well as Christophe. I don't need to let patients hug me like Christophe, but mostly they need to feel accepted and free of judgment in my presence."

On this topic of unconditional love and acceptance, Brenda shares how dogs have helped stop her from imposing "shoulds" on herself, and to be more accepting of others unconditionally.

"Being able to love unconditionally and ending my judgmental habits comes with my journey of accepting my illness with MS, after being progressively more disabled in my physical capabilities. For a long time, being paralyzed, in my chair, on my vent, I had felt I should be doing more for people, at least carrying my own weight, and therefore I judged myself as deficient. But learning from dogs, working with them to visit patients, I realized my presence alone was enough. People needed my loving presence at least as much as anything else. If I had been more physically able to move around and busier, I would not have focused so much on offering my full acceptance and compassion to others. Now I finally believe there is a reason I have had MS—to make me a true comforter. It has focused me on what I have to give to others—my heart, my time, my ears, my empathy. And when I go into a room with my dogs and visit people at the end of their lives, I can just be free to love them."

Brenda and Don are highly involved with the local hospice. In their hospice visits, they practice their quiet, unconditional love along with their dogs, allowing the visit to provide a peaceful sanctuary for people in the last days of their lives. Don tenderly reflects on his experiences in hospices:

"We have witnessed powerful experiences of comforting when we bring our dogs to hospice care. For patients at the end of their lives, dogs can help a family say good-bye. Often the patient will invite the dog to come up on the bed with them. The dog lies comfortably next to the patient, so when a family member sits or stands by the bed, they can pat the dog and talk to the dog, especially when they are having difficulty speaking with their loved one who is dying. Dogs help the patient and family handle the long silences that can feel empty and awkward.

"Family members often feel a sense of relief when they see the dog resting against the patient, feeling the closeness and comfort of the dog. The dog serves as a kind of hub of love for family and friends, as they connect to the patient through the dog, telling stories, sharing news, or just quietly enjoying the dog, stroking the fur, getting their hands licked, and sitting together in a tender moment."

What Dogs Teach Us About Comforting

DON AND BRENDA SUMMARIZED THE KEY WAYS DOGS TEACH COMFORTERS:

- When we don't know what to say at awkward times, dogs give us something in common to talk about—about themselves, about other dogs or other pets, or about where their owners have taken them.

- Dogs help us handle long silences together, especially when we are in a comforting role with someone in pain or distress. Dogs encourage us to allow more silence, to relax, to feel free from having to talk or entertain someone.

- The contagious energy of dogs can calm us on hectic days and perk us up on dreary days.

- Their empathy is powerful, as they feel strongly what we feel, reflecting back to us the truth and depth of our own feelings.

- They slow us down, keep us grounded, and invite us to be in the present moment.

- When we are in pain, they can distract and engage us and draw our attention away from our fears and our worries.

- Dogs remind us we are never really alone, no matter how lonely we feel.

- Dogs help us cut through social pretenses, our status, or the inflation of our egos, or "BS," and to be humble and authentic. They are great levelers—equalizers for humans.

- Dogs help life feel normal in abnormal situations.

- When medical staff have to break bad news, dogs can be a comfort for the patient and for the family members in the room.

- Dogs can draw out affection and love from withdrawn, depressed, or disoriented people, especially patients in clinical settings.

- Dogs also help focus and orient elders with cognitive disabilities, with dementia or Alzheimer's, or those who have had strokes.

Comforting Suggestions for Families or Other Groups

With your own dog or a borrowed dog, Don and Brenda suggest the following comforting activities we can do with dogs:

- Enjoying some quiet time brushing and grooming them
- Playing with their toys, with balls, sticks and Frisbees, and getting down on the ground to play
- Watching pets playing together and laughing at their goofy stuff
- Observing pets comfort and nurture each other
- Holding your pets, loving them
- Taking walks and exploring with them
- Enjoying all their little routines; their predictability is comforting
- Reading stories and seeing movies and TV shows about animals and nature, which can be fun to share and talk about

. ❦ .

HORSE WISDOM: CLARITY AND FIRMNESS FOR COMFORTERS

Nancy Coyne, M.D.

Staff Psychiatrist and Instructor

Epona Center for Equine Experiential Learning

Sonoita, Arizona

Thirty years in private practice as a psychiatrist

specializing in treating trauma survivors

We don't have to be mean to mean what we say. Horses teach us how to be clear and firm, balanced with gentleness and respect.

Core Comforting Qualities: Clarity and Strength

Nancy Coyne has had thirty years' experience in private practice with trauma survivors, working with victims of domestic violence as well as veterans with PTSD. Yet for all the grief and pain she has known in listening to the stories of her clients' harsh lives, she is deeply hopeful, an old soul, with a wonderful smile and a generous heart.

About ten years ago, she began to focus her practice more on working with horses as healers after she had observed how people who were devastated by human violence naturally connected with animals. She believed many survivors needed other-than-human connections to heal from human-caused trauma. Several years ago, inspired by the brilliant work of Linda Kohanov, Nancy moved to Arizona to work at the Epona Center for Equine Experiential Learning, which Linda had founded. Now as one of Epona's instructors and their staff psychiatrist, Nancy counsels different groups of survivors, including veterans returning from Iraq and Afghanistan, survivors of domestic abuse and child abuse, and other survivors of violent crime.

Nancy is full of life because she loves her life, dedicated to her soul's calling of working with horses as healers. She lives most of the year on her seven-acre farm near Sonoita, Arizona, with her partner, four horses, one donkey, one mini horse, two llamas, two goats, two cats, and two dogs.

She migrates to Maine every summer to work with her East Coast clients and teach workshops. She spends her leisure time riding her horse in the desert near her farm. She speaks exuberantly of this experience: "Exquisite comfort comes from being one with the horse I am riding, a sense of being synchronized, and knowing the horse picks up on what I want with my slightest movements, tuning in to me. The horse and I work in such tandem that we both feel a freedom of movement, as if we are the same organism, breathing together the essence of the same life force."

Her love and reverence for horses began with one of her earliest experiences on a horse when she was at camp as a young girl. As the sun was about to rise, she had secretly taken off on a horse from the stable, leaving the camp to ride bareback alone through a nearby field. She had immersed herself in the freedom and wildness of her adventurous ride, but soon she fell off her horse. As she lay on the ground, her horse gently kept from crushing her, placing his foot carefully on her belly. Amazed, she looked up, eye to eye with her horse, who protectively gazed down at her. This moment of trust and soulful connection has stayed with her all her life.

She shared another more recent story about a horse named Samson, a great comforting friend of hers who appeared at Epona a few years ago.

"I was grieving deeply over issues in my family and feeling lonely and teary. One day at Epona ranch a big black draft horse named Samson arrived in Arizona all the way from Michigan. This was his first day in Arizona, and we expected him to be restless and agitated. As I approached the fence, he trotted up and reached his head over the fence to me. Before I knew it, my face was buried in his neck, and he let me hug him for quite a while. We were all surprised. It was as if he felt what was in my heart, and feeling displaced and nervous himself, he came to me. It was mutual comforting."

I wondered about the particular qualities of horses that were comforting for trauma survivors, as opposed to the comfort of dogs, for example. Nancy answered this easily.

"Horses are different than dogs in what they teach us about comforting. Dogs are quite forthcoming with their love and attention—they dish it out! Horses, unlike dogs, require certain qualities from us, especially our careful attunement, because they are so much bigger than dogs and bigger than us. They are also prey animals, used to running from predators, and have been mistreated by humans for millenniums, so horses are highly sensitive to our gentleness, patience, and respect. However, they need our clarity and firmness, too, in guiding them."

"So horses need us to be very soft and careful with them, respectful, but also to be clear and firm." I said this out loud, letting the words sink in.

Nancy was eager to explain this. "This softness, balanced with clarity and firmness, is so important for trauma survivors to learn. This is a soft kind of strength that means being powerful without being demanding. People who have been traumatized by violence mistakenly think they have to be mean to mean what they say. They have learned strength and power in destructive experiences of force and aggression. Horses show us ways to be powerful through our presence, our focus, our belief, our energetic conviction behind our words. We need to be clear with horses in what we want them to do and what we want ourselves to do. Horses need our boundaries and capacities made quite obvious. For people who have been abused or violated in some way, horses draw out of them an ability to say no or yes with solid conviction, strong boundaries, or else the horse will stray or pull away from the rider's intentions."

"Don't these horses intimidate some of your clients?" I wondered.

"Many of the horses at Epona are abused animals themselves, some retired racehorses, who still want to be useful and active but need our support. The trauma survivors and abused horses bond well together because they sense each other's wounds, each other's sensitivity, shyness, and hesitancy to make connections. They both need lots of gentleness, softness, and slow gradual steps to trusting each other. Some of the most important work happens before the survivors ever get on the horses, by taking time getting to know each other through brushing, grooming, cleaning, and leading the horses on walks, or in feeding them. They grow attached and little signs of communication are developed."

Though dogs will approach almost anyone with affection,

horses, more discriminating, will choose the people they like, and clients soon realize they are special in some unique way for their horse. Nancy continues, "Every day I hear clients exclaim how good it feels when they are *chosen* by a certain horse. It boosts their spirits, not just their self-esteem, when they say, "Look, he walked right up to me. He nuzzled me. He really likes me!" Horses quickly show us what sensitive qualities they need from us, but they definitely must have our clear direction and boundaries. They will test our limits and our patience, and we must be steady, calm, and determined."

Nancy's comments stirred some old, die-hard beliefs still inside me about how our softness, gentleness, and patience as comforters could be exploited by others. If we were empathic and generous with each other, without boundaries and clarity, we could get sucked into being too submissive, too available to others, or self-sacrificing. I and many highly empathic people I knew, especially when I was younger, had struggled with our softheartedness, as controlling people tried to take advantage of us. Boundaries, firmness, and clarity seemed to go against the ingrained images of comforters in our minds, as our softer, comforting qualities seemed opposed to the "real world" qualities of toughness, guile, and dominance. Softness was still equated with weakness, subservience, and gullibility in our culture, so we empathic types were forced to go against our true natures, to be wary of our softheartedness to protect ourselves. Trauma survivors, especially of abuse, were extremely guarded against their softer, compassionate attributes that previously may have misled them to forgiving and tolerating their perpetrators. Many trauma survivors couldn't risk being soft in a world that was still hard to be soft in—where bullying, controlling people still thrived in many workplaces, schools, courts, or on the streets. And because their softness had gotten them in trouble with relationships, they hardened themselves, often to their own detriment, and missed out on opportunities to be comforting.

Yet Nancy was saying we didn't have to become hardened in order to be hard sometimes, and horses showed us the grace of this truth. Horses proved to us we did not have to completely let down our guard to be soft and comforting. We could sustain good boundaries and be clear and firm about our availability, and *still* be soft as comforters. She offered, by way of the wisdom of horses, a fresh perspective for comforters to reconcile our softness with our strength. Indeed, horses taught us the power of soft strength.

What Horses Teach Us as Comforters and Healers
Nancy shares the most important things horses can teach us:

- Horses don't lie. We learn to be scrupulously honest with ourselves and others.
- Horses are mirrors of our emotions and behaviors. If we have been denying or neglecting to face truths about ourselves, horses will reveal what we need to observe. Horses teach comforters to be aware of their own vulnerabilities and limitations, before approaching someone in distress,

or else they might get pulled into actions they would regret later.

- Horses lower our blood pressure and calm us down.
- Horses teach us to be keenly aware of our environment and our effects on our environment.
- Horses teach us to be clear and firm as comforters, but not at the expense of our gentler, softer qualities.

· ❧ ·

THE COMFORT OF CONTINUITY:
RITUALS, ROUTINES, AND SEASONS

Laura Hare
Children's center director for thirty years; creator of nature programs for children
Former Director, The Growing Tree
Richmond, Virginia

Our pets especially teach us the comfort of continuity, as they are creatures of habit who find great joy in the most mundane daily routines with us.

Core Comforting Qualities: Reliability and Patience

Laura greets me at the front door of her little lavender bungalow bedecked with window boxes full of pansies. A swinging chair with yellow cushions hangs on her front porch in the cool shade. She quickly closes the door behind me so her cats don't run out, then gives me a big hug. She eagerly leads me to her back lawn to the tiny pond she built by several old apple trees. She points to her amazingly hardy "Terminator" goldfish in the pond, who have survived predators, ice storms, droughts, and heat waves. Next she shows me her cozy patio with potted geraniums, and then takes me to her sunroom with wide arched windows, where the evening sun streams through her crystals and across her hanging baskets of ivy.

She invites me to sit in a well-cushioned old wicker chair and hands me an iced tea. I sip it down quickly, under her wide ceiling fan on this balmy June evening in Richmond, Virginia.

Laura sits back snugly on her blue gingham sofa with her two black cats, on either side of her lap, watching every move I make.

In her cat's astute glare, I glance self-consciously around her room, admiring her handiwork, her country quilts and throws, painted floral cabinets, baskets of seashells, and then happily remember our plans for tomorrow.

"Laura, we are definitely going to Charles City Tavern tomorrow?"

"It's a go—I can't wait." She shakes her head in amazement. "Wow . . . I can't believe it's been a year since I've seen you." She hoots out loud and reaches across the coffee table to give me a high five. "Charles City Tavern tomorrow!" Annoyed with all the attention I am getting, her cats jump off the couch in protest, but don't get farther than the doorway, where they lie down, their backs toward us, feigning they aren't listening.

Throughout our twenty-five-year friendship, Laura and I have kept sacred our pilgrimage to Charles City on the lush, green banks of the James River east of Richmond. We adore this old, gracious tavern, and always sit on the screened porch next to an herb garden, enjoying our Saturday midafternoon lunch, finishing it with our usual bourbon-soaked pecan pie with vanilla ice cream for dessert. Afterward, happily dazed in a sugar rush, we stroll amid the willow trees, pink roses, and irises all swaying in the moist, salty breezes streaming from the flat fields of soy and peanuts for miles around us.

Our ritual at Charles City Tavern has become increasingly more meaningful over the past ten years, ever since I moved away to Maine. If Laura and I lived to our eighties, even if the tavern fell into ruins, we'd still be walking along the James River every June for our annual reunion. I've always been able to count on Laura, and more than most friends and colleagues, she values the role of rituals, the magic of keeping reunions going, even for decades. Laura has always been the one to rely on, to show up for the life passages, great or small, for the people she loves. She honors the continuity of events with everyone in her life, from her family members, to the children she teaches, to her friends and colleagues.

This Friday evening we talk for a long time, almost to midnight, about Laura's understanding of the art of comforting. In a nutshell for her, it's all about sustaining continuity in our relationships. We need our reunions, our rituals, our little routines and cycles, especially children. Nature teaches this always, through the tides, moons, migrations, seasons, and generations we share with all of creation.

L AURA HAS DIRECTED children's programs for twenty-eight years, teaching life skills through a better understanding of the cycles and ways of nature. She's always had a knack for creating routines and rituals that make kids look forward to activities and roles. Whether it's getting kids psyched for a Halloween Spook Night, cleaning Muffy the turtle's tank, awaiting the birth of more bunnies from Stewey and Petunia, navigating maps for camping trips, or planting a cherry tree, she brilliantly taps the power of their anticipation and suspense.

Laura previously specialized in working with children with disabilities, launching one of the first community inclusion initiatives in Virginia for after-school and recreational programs that integrated children with disabilities into mainstream activities. Her highly successful program at the Growing Tree in Richmond became the actual model for the Everybuddy Program of the Chesterfield public school system.

At the heart of her success in integrating children with disabilities with other children in the mainstream is her practice of bringing nature and animals into her learning places. Everyone plays an important role, as each child is responsible for caring for their chosen animal, their plant, or their garden. When they take on the role of caregivers, a leveling process is established for all children, no matter how academically successful or not, how popular or not, or how deprived or not a child's background may be. No one is any better than anyone else, but everyone is equally accountable for what they do in nurturing the animals who depend on them.

Grounded by rituals and routines, kids learn by continuity, Laura attests. Things we learn certainly sink in better when we watch over time how life moves in cycles, how habits form, and how people commit to work together. Further, continuity is deeply reassuring, a foundation for facing loss and change in life. In the face of life transitions, it's important to keep some things as continuous as possible, whether it's having dinner together at the same time of evening, or walking the dogs, or doing laundry every Saturday. "But continuity requires our reliability and keeping commitments. We've got to be able to count on each other, or else we learn *not* to count on each other, and lose our faith in our promises, to each other as well as ourselves. Kids are so beautiful when they light up with anticipation for a big event, when they are counting on everyone to show up, but with too many no-shows, they lose their spirit, get discouraged, cynical. It's easy to understand why some of them turn too much to technology, to computers, video games, TV, and virtual worlds for continuity in their lives," Laura says with a sigh.

Laura isn't against technology, but she worries that we aren't learning essential comforting skills if we get too caught up in the instant gratification of "following" people on cell phones, BlackBerry phones, and Twitter. Instant gratification in quick cell calls and social networking can't teach us the slower, gentler, mostly nonverbal language of comforting. And virtual people can't touch us, hold us.

Laura continues, "Technology is important and has its place, but I believe humans are starving for the same direct attention our pets crave. With animals, being their only virtual buddies doesn't do the trick. Our pets will die of loneliness without our hands-on affection, smiles, voices, hugs, and play time. And by play time, I mean getting down on our hands and knees, being silly, making crazy sounds, roughhousing a bit. And, I dare say, too many of the kids I teach and their *parents* are lonely for these same comforts."

Nurturing animals and the earth creates continuity in our lives, as others depend on us to grow and survive. We are hardwired to nurture other living beings, and we often don't realize this until we discover the joys of taking care of even the smallest of creatures. Laura reminisced on her childhood farm experiences and how she tries to bring similar experiences to children in her work today.

"I learned the wisdom and comfort of nature from my childhood experiences on my grandparents' farm in the rolling hills of western Virginia. To this day, I carry inside me the blessings of growing up with the freedom to jump into haystacks, climb oak trees, and play in our tree houses.

We swam in a large pond fed by a bubbling stream, and napped on warm moss under weeping willow trees. We canned beans, peaches, and tomatoes and pickled cucumbers. We tended a two-acre vegetable garden and picked apples, pears, and peaches from our plentiful orchards. We nurtured baby chicks and ducklings and played with dozens of dogs and cats. Looking back, I realize I was very, very fortunate to have spent so many idyllic years learning about life on a farm.

"But further, this wisdom of nature was ultimately comforting for me. Children can better understand loss, even death, with nature, when they witness the life cycles, seasons, the frailty as well as resilience of living beings. Knowing that life goes on, no matter what, is comforting. Knowing that nature always has something to teach us, even in loss, is comforting.

"Today, as a child care director, I have built educational programs inspired by the wisdom and comfort of the animals of my life and my years at my grandparents' farm."

Laura's Comforting Practices
Teaching Comforting Skills with Nature at the Growing Tree
At Laura's Growing Tree program, the children each cared for their own animal. Inherent in the act of caregiving were ideal opportunities to practice comforting skills, to develop a strong sense of continuity, belonging, teamwork, and community over the years.

HERE ARE THE MOST IMPORTANT COMFORTING QUALITIES
CHILDREN HAVE LEARNED, BY BUILDING RELATIONSHIPS
WITH THEIR PETS AND PLANTS:

Reliability

If Swimmy the goldfish doesn't get his meals on time,
he gets into fights with the other fish and causes trouble in
the tank. To keep harmony in the tank, feeding times have
to be consistent, so we need to be dependable for feeding
Swimmy.

Empathy

When Louie the cockatiel is upset and squawking, the
children stop whatever they are doing and listen to
him, to tune in to him so they can understand what is
upsetting him.

Gentleness, Patience, Calmness

If Louie is still squawking, the children quiet down,
slow down, and gently step closer to him to see what he
needs to calm down. They lower their voices and speak
softly to him. If a child is putting her hands in his cage to
add water when Louie is nervous, she needs to patiently,
delicately pick up his little water bowl.

Presence

If Muffy the turtle is slowly inching her way through
the room, we need to be very careful where we put our

feet. If we hold Stewey and Petunia's tiny baby rabbits, we must be attentive and focus closely, as they are fragile and need our utmost care.

Respect and Appreciation

If Petunia is tired and resting with her babies who are sleeping, we need to respect her needs and leave them alone for a while. We would not disturb Petunia by petting her or picking her up for a cuddle.

Caring

When Muffy the turtle became very ill with a bacterial infection, Laura and the children decided to try to save Muffy by carefully giving her a series of injections into her tiny legs. A child was chosen to hold Muffy steadily while Laura administered the injections for several days. The children gathered every day to watch closely this delicate treatment. Though Muffy nearly died, she did come through finally and lived another seven years afterward.

Clarity and Boundaries

It would be confusing and stressful for Oreo the guinea pig to have the whole yard to run in for one day, and then be kept in his cage for another day. Oreo's caregivers all need to uphold the same rules and behaviors and be unified in how and where they play with him.

Comforting in Times of Loss: Louie's Stones and Whitney's Tree

In caring for animals, the children sometimes faced loss and death, and learned to comfort themselves and each other when providing memorial ceremonies for their pets.

When Louie the cockatiel died of old age, the children laid him in a shoe box, wrapped carefully in a doll's blanket with his favorite things—his bell, his whistle, and some birdseed. He was buried at the end of the backyard, inside a circle of small stones by a bush. For his funeral, the children sang songs, read poems, and shared memories in his honor.

A year later, a girl named Whitney from the Growing Tree program suddenly and tragically died in a boating accident with her father the day after Valentine's Day. Laura met with the children at the Growing Tree and talked about Whitney's death in an honest, sensitive way. After remembering in great detail what they had done for Louie's funeral, the children suggested planting a tree for Whitney and designed a ceremony.

A few weeks later, a cherry tree was planted in the front yard of the Growing Tree as a memorial ceremony for Whitney's family members and her fellow students. The children, Laura, other staff, and Whitney's family members all held hands and made a circle around Whitney's cherry tree after it was planted and offered prayers and blessings. The children shared their poems, pictures, and Whitney's favorite songs.

Over the years, Whitney's tree has grown strong and tall, and many former students of the Growing Tree, now adults, stop by to remember her.

Laura's Comforting Suggestions for Families

As a child care director, Laura observes that families need to gather together on a regular basis to keep the art of comforting alive. Essentially, we can create our own traditions, our own memory-makers.

- Great family traditions, rituals, memory-makers

    Children tell Laura constantly what traditions they enjoy, especially events centered on nature, animals, or the seasons. They love it when adults make these events special, meaningful, memorable. The simplest activity can be turned into a rewarding ritual together.

HERE ARE SOME FAVORITE ACTIVITIES WITH ANIMALS AND NATURE THAT CHILDREN TALK ABOUT FOR YEARS AND YEARS:

- Getting out the plastic swimming (wading) pool, or turning on the sprinklers at the start of the summer to play in the water is a ritual in itself! Pool parties can be an annual tradition (often around Memorial Day). Getting out the lounge chairs, the hammock, or the deck chairs to sit outside or on the porch.
- Going on a picnic or a day trip to a favorite natural park or local sandy beach (by a lake, river, or ocean) in the warmer seasons. Take photos, too.

- Birthday parties for our pets, or parties for their special occasions, including playing games with their toys and watching them play.
- Playing Frisbee or other ball game with our dogs, family, and friends in the backyard or the park on the weekends.
- A show-and-tell event for sharing the stories and pictures of our pets or of other animals we have known or loved (dog stories, cat stories, horse stories, gerbil stories . . .). Also, we can create show-and-tell events after completing any special environmental projects, such as going to the park to clean up trash and debris, or doing other community service projects for our environment.
- Planting seeds in the spring for gardens, window boxes, or indoor plants. Tree-planting ceremonies.
- Making an annual video or movie of a favorite activity with our pets, to enjoy later as a follow-up event with popcorn.

OTHER TRADITIONS AND RITUALS

- A regular sports event (seasonal) to attend together. Even the trip to the stadium can be a ritual in itself.
- A monthly Saturday or Sunday movie matinee, with an after-movie bite to eat, to talk about the movie or just visit.
- A trip to a museum for a special exhibit.
- Going to annual parades, participating in parades.
- A trip to a historic landmark.
- Fashion shows with fun clothing or costumes, set to lively music so we can strut down the "catwalk."
- Going to the library for story hour with a brown-bag lunch.

- Every fall, or for Thanksgiving, loading up cans of food to donate to the local food bank.

· ❦ ·

THE RADIANCE OF STILLNESS

Jen Deraspe

Director and Owner, Nurture Through Nature,

an eco-retreat center in Denmark, Maine

We ask ourselves, "How can I connect with nature?" as if we've forgotten we already are a part of nature. We are nature–as much as any tree, flower, or bird. If we take a moment to be still and quiet, we can reconnect with the source of all life through sacred silence.

Core Comforting Qualities: Stillness and Presence

On a mission to write my column, "Leaps of Faith," for the *Maine Women's Journal* two years ago, I drove to interview Jen at her retreat center in western Maine. I passed through mountains glowing in autumn foliage, flowing rapids, and deep blue lakes before reaching a cluster of cabins in the pines off a dirt road. I stepped out of my car in splendidly rugged wilderness, in scenery that guests like me hoped to find when they came from Boston, New York, or even Portland, Maine. Jen quickly and warmly greeted me and led me to her largest cabin, where she pointed out her dining and communal areas and showed me one of the guest rooms. I was struck by the elegant simplicity of the golden red pinewood floors, tables, and walls, and the radiant fresh-picked wildflowers and ferns. Her woodstove provided toasty heat by the table we chose for our interview. Jen poured me and herself a cup of peppermint tea from a blue teapot. Looking across the table, I spotted a striking photograph of a white owl.

"That owl gives me a chill, a good kind of chill," I told Jen. "I love the eyes, those soulful eyes, so much awareness in those eyes."

Jen sat back, paused, and smiled lovingly at the owl picture. "It is a beautiful shot, isn't it?"

"Really, really is . . . Who took the photo?" I asked eagerly.

"Don't know . . . I don't think I've ever known." She seemed perfectly content not knowing. We enjoyed a moment of stillness, in reverence of the owl's eyes.

"We can hear owls not too far from here," she added softly.

Jen put me at ease as we shared other bird encounters with blue herons and hawks. We held our mugs of steaming tea, gazing through the window as the wind lifted and coaxed the orange and yellow leaves off their trees. Autumn demanded our attention and we welcomed its presence. Soon, looking back at Jen checking the logs piled beside her woodstove, my curiosity got me going again, and I asked her about her background.

Having a passion for health and wellness, Jen got her master's degree in sports medicine and served on the faculty and as the head athletic trainer for the University of Southern Maine for ten years, taking care of the health care needs of the college athletes. Over time, she felt compelled to work with people in a more holistic way, including nature as a pathway toward stillness and healing. In that realization, she resigned from that line of work and began her own business, Nurture Through Nature, offering holistic canoe retreats for women, yoga instruction, and holistic personal training services. During that transition time, she earned her Maine guide's license as well as her certification to be a yoga instructor. She found a mentor who worked with her to find stillness in her own busy mind and tendency to strive and drive hard and fast. In releasing her own distress, she got excited about sharing the possibilities found in peace. Along the journey, she found The Work of Byron Katie to be a direct path toward inner peace and freedom and became a facilitator of The Work of Byron Katie.

With her versatile background, Jen could provide a holistic assortment of activities at her center through mindfulness eco-retreats. In the past year, she was focusing more on custom workshops "devoted to inner peace and presence," facilitating retreats to "grow our own souls" and sharing The Work of Byron Katie as a means toward more clarity and less stress. She also accommodated custom retreats for those groups or couples who designed their own program, and hosted solo retreats for guests who simply wanted to spend private time in her woodland sanctuary.

Jen's ability to invite moments of stillness and quietude, even during my first interview with her, inspired me to get to know her later as a colleague and as a master comforter. Clearly, Jen was a gentle teacher gifted at guiding us to enter our precious center, creating sacred pauses for our lives. She describes a powerful, profound experience in her life when facing the death of her brother as a child, and finding comfort in a moment of deep stillness—a moment that taught her the meaning of comfort.

"I was eight years old when my older brother died. In the first days after his death, my father rocked me in his arms for a long time in the fading light of our family room, and we said nothing. The memory of this silent and deeply loving experience has stayed with me ever since, teaching me the power of what 'being there'—being here, not 'there'—really means for being human. I truly honor silence and stillness, how offering this for each other is essential for tapping our heart's language, to be able to drop down into the embrace of our own hearts. Whether we give hugs or just sit softly with someone, our warmth is there when we allow sacred pause for our hearts to speak."

More recently Jen has given me her time to explore more deeply the topic of comforting, especially the comfort of nature. I was keen on hearing what she thought about our societal disconnection from nature, and how this might interfere with our ability to be comforting.

I was surprised by her answer. "We ask ourselves, 'How can I connect with nature?' as if we've forgotten we *already are* a part of nature. We *are* nature—as much as any tree, flower, or bird. We don't always have to go outdoors. If we take a moment to be still and quiet, we can reconnect with the source of all life through sacred silence."

"So stillness and quiet give us a chance for nature to comfort us," I echoed.

"Stillness can be radiant. We pause and see how vibrant life is around us. How nature speaks to us."

I completely agreed with Jen. "Yes, though we know this is true, we shortchange ourselves most of the time by doing too much and missing out on savoring the gifts of the moment."

"Absolutely," Jen continued. "This is why I've started a more radical practice to make myself stop and be quiet for at least one minute every hour, for most hours of the day. It's really quite simple and deliberate with the aid of technology—my watch! My watch has a timer that I can set to go off every hour, and it has this sweet little chime that lets me know it's time to stop whatever I am doing and pause. So, when my watch chimes, it's time for my moment of silence. I allow a whole sixty seconds to be quiet and come back to the present. And this is not just for me anymore. It is downright comforting when that chime time comes! Talk about 'saved by the bell!' I get caught in the middle of doing things, and after a moment of silence, I realize how unpresent I have been in the moment."

I listened closely as Jen spoke. She added, "Even though we yearn to be in the wilderness, to enjoy the beauty of a forest or a mountain, we quickly notice how our minds are distracted with nagging thoughts we have carried with us from home, keeping us from being comforted by the serenity of our surroundings. These inner distractions keep us from simply being present to ourselves and who or what is in front of us."

It struck me how important it is for us to be in a receptive mode in nature, to free our minds from the thicket of our busy thoughts. Walking, yoga, or canoeing certainly gave us the methods to wind our minds down, doing a concrete, physical activity, allowing us to ground our bodies, dropping into our bodies and hearts, away from those hyper-speeding zones of the mind. Even twenty minutes of a good walk on a path in the woods could shift our thinking into calmer awareness. The whole world could look different to us after a walk under the pines, and we might notice the brilliant goldfinches hopping on the branches right ahead of us. And if we had a loved one with us, stopping in the morning light to enjoy the gold glory of the finches, we shared a true moment of comfort.

"So, Jen, your role in this process is to facilitate people learning to be quiet enough and grounded enough to receive the comfort of nature. You teach us how to open up and be present to what the earth has to teach us."

"Yes. And it works both ways—as we open ourselves to our natural surroundings, we learn the other-than-human languages of life around us—the language of animals, of seasons, of the wind, of the skies and waters, of mountains . . . of stillness. With more stillness, we begin to tap in to the wise voice within. And sacred silence."

I chimed in. "I see what you mean—we need to be willing to be still, to be present to these languages of creation around us, and step out of our own terms, beyond words."

Jen nodded and added, "Here's an example of what we might call 'tree language': I love to watch how one of my favorite trees stays so rooted and strong while bending against the storms. The roots teach me how to stay grounded and rooted when a perceived storm arrives in myself or another. I remember my roots, all the things that keep me grounded—my home, my local community, my loved ones, my work. I can reflect on the tree's roots before I offer comfort to someone in distress."

With Jen, I didn't need to rush to any clever comments to cheer up our pensive moment. I sat still in our silence, remembering my favorite trees in my life. Yes, sitting under a majestic two-hundred-year-old oak tree was more than just sitting. We could tap the strength of those roots with our quietude and stillness, taking a deep breath and beholding their steadfast power. And then we could carry this tree's presence with us when we set out to comfort a person in pain.

Jen's Comforting Practices with Groups

Since 1999, Jen has consistently and successfully been providing retreats and gatherings, and facilitating workshops to help people slow down, soften, and quiet themselves. Highly skilled in helping her retreaters transition gently from their busier lives into a retreat's simpler, more mindful ways, she lists suggestions here that can be widely applied in other group settings, including at home:

A Welcoming Atmosphere: Music, Food, Drinks, and Flowers
Warm and relaxing music, easy-access food or potluck offerings, and even the simplest flower arrangements quickly contribute to a comforting environment. Basically, these are the welcoming signs that set the stage for gathering together, conveying the message, "Come join us. You are welcome here." Jen describes her beautiful ritual for preparing for her guests:

> "To prepare for an upcoming retreat, and to connect with my heart energy, I enjoy a simple ritual of placing flowers in vases for the tables and bedrooms of our center. I can't help but smile and feel myself softening as the flowers beam back their beauty to me in the morning light. Next I put on some gentle music and light a circle of candles. I walk around the candles, in unison with footsteps and music. When my guests start arriving, I am ready to share my presence, coming from the sweetness of the flowers, music, and candles, and sincerely greet each retreat guest."

The Role as Facilitator or Host

At the beginning of her retreats, Jen warmly greets her guests and welcomes them to the retreat space. She briefly shares with her group her background and what drew her to her work, and how she will facilitate the retreat's activities.

She states it is very comforting for guests to understand the parameters of her role and how she is available. Essentially, this serves as an orientation to help participants "get their bearings" and feel at home.

In broader applications, the role of any host or facilitator is to graciously greet guests and assist in orienting them. This provides a sense of belonging, which is reassuring and inviting. Let guests know what is available, what is planned, who is available (the "go-to" people), and where things are. The role of a host (or hosts) is a vital comforting role, as people attending need to know what is going on and how they can get assistance if they need it.

Greeters and hosts (the warm and sometimes fuzzy "go-to" people) are essential for comforting experiences for groups, especially when there are newcomers. Team meetings at work start off better with a sincere welcome by an appointed host, expressing appreciation for people showing up. Even family and friends gatherings need at least one greeter as people wander through the doorway.

What We Are Grateful for Today

Jen believes talking about what we are grateful for is a great icebreaker for a gathering, especially before a meal, or at the start of an event. Retreat guests readily share their observations of what they are grateful for in the past day or week, and this naturally invites comfortable conversation.

Likewise, any participant at any kind of gathering, a meeting, a party, a book club, can share this warm-up topic.

Sharing Our Intentions

Retreat guests state what brought them to the event, and what they hope to gain from the experience. They are free to disclose as little or as much as they like about why they wanted to participate in the event.

For wider applications, at early stages of meetings and gatherings, it's comforting for people to state what brought them together and what they hope to gain from the experience, though this information is offered voluntarily.

Reading Poems or Blessings, or Saying Prayers

A short poem, a thoughtful blessing, or a centering prayer all focus people on the goal or the inspiration for an event. It helps get everyone "on the same page," with beautiful, heartening words.

Outdoor Exercise

Outdoors, Jen leads exercises to help guests find comfort in nature. She says to people, "Walk as if you are kissing the earth with your feet, stepping softly and lightly upon your mother's back." She encourages people to walk while allowing themselves to feel fully with their feet what they are walking through. She leads a walking meditation along a mountain brook path. She also leads yoga exercises outside, so guests can open up their bodies and spirits to the wide sky above them and the soft mossy earth below them.

Her guests over the years have especially loved an exercise of finding a special spot in the woods, where they can sit by themselves and reflect on a particular question about their lives. Before locating this special spot, Jen facilitates their ability to follow their instincts in the wilderness:

> "Let the space call you to it—you can sense the right spot for you and follow it. It might be a certain tree, or a shady glen or a clearing by a meadow. Sit with what has drawn you in to it—what was it about this spot that called you? How does this space feel to you? Quiet? Vibrant? Soft? Fierce? How does this space affect the way you are looking at your life situation now?"

She asks her guests to describe their interaction with their special spot and their question. Many comment they didn't feel so alone anymore with their burden or with their problem. Retreat-goers often noticed that the spaces beckoning them symbolically reflected a certain aspect of their lives that needed examining.

For example, someone drawn to a stream in a shady glen might have wanted to reflect on aspects of flow and opportunities in their lives, when they were feeling fearful of "going with the flow."

As individuals on our own, we can apply this exercise with walks in the natural world. We can allow ourselves to be "called" to a certain spot with which we feel a special affinity. Often the terrain and setting we choose for our resting spot might just speak to us, give us messages in sounds, smells, images, symbols, sensations. If we just sit and open ourselves to the present moment, something might beckon us to study it and learn from it.

Jen's Invitations to Exploring Comforting Activities Together
Jen suggests, "Experiment with spending more time in nature and sensing how this feels. Try being unplugged from media and technology for a spell and notice the contrast." I reflect on what Jen said as I watch children playing outside my window, on a large lawn next door, bordered by apple and pine trees and a little fountain. Four of them, under ten years of age, are having a blast, chasing each other and shrieking exuberantly. What a joy to behold! I smile, knowing these kids have found the great treasures of running wildly in the long golden light of evening. The chickadees are singing their mating songs while the children race along the stone fences, laughing. Spring is here. It just doesn't get any better than this.

Jen also suggests a few other activities:

"Make sacred pauses throughout the day. At least a few times during the day, take a minute or two just to stop, breathe, and come fully back into the present moment.

"Do exercises or yoga outside, even just walking. When we move our bodies outdoors, we may breathe better and sleep better at night.

"Play games outdoors, or on the porch, even card games are fun when sitting on a blanket on the grass. When we are outdoors, our sense of spaciousness and perspective is expanded. Stepping away from our ceilings and walls can open up our minds, and then our hearts.

"Have picnics and eat outdoors, or even on the porch. Find little spots where you can sit alone, in a garden, or the woods, or a park. Having alone time with nature quickly reminds us we are never really alone. There is life around us, and creation speaks to us.

"Go barefoot on the ground whenever you can. It can bring out the best of us as humans, just digging our feet in the warm sand or stepping into a cool spring. Happy feet can tell us it's good to be alive!"

CHAPTER 9

Self-Comforting for Comforters

Renewing Our Compassion

EVEN THE MOST EMPATHIC, GENEROUS, and kindhearted people among us experience compassion fatigue at times. In our yearning to be effective comforters, we often forget that we are only human beings, with human limitations. As much as we would love to keep going strong like the Energizer Bunny, we can simply run out of comfort to give.

Those of us in human services, health care, pastoral care, education, and other caregiver fields face compassion fatigue on a regular basis, and though we may vent privately that we are "sick of suffering fools," or "fed up with ungrateful jerks," many of us never let go of our drive to constantly "be there" for people who need us. In my work as a counselor in behavioral health and hospice settings, I certainly battled bouts of despair and pessimism about the state of the world, let alone how useless I felt to protect others from its harsh realities. And as much as I believed wholeheartedly in remaining compassionate toward others each and every day—maintaining my regimens for stress management, work/life balance, and good boundaries—my supply of comfort often come up short.

In this chapter I will share some of the wisdom I've gained from my own experiences as well as from other comforters on how to take care of yourself even when you're taking care of others.

FINDING STRENGTH IN COMMUNITY

Over the years I've been blessed with colleagues and friends who have heartened me when I've doubted my own capacity to be a comforter. These gifted individuals were able to sit down and give me the support I needed at crucial moments, working wonders with my compassion fatigue. But these comforting people didn't just show up at my doorstep, my kitchen table, or my desk at work. I had to work to find them.

Sometimes our friends and family members are just too overwhelmed to lift us out of our own compassion fatigue. Though we may have relied on them for comfort in the past, in stressful and demanding times, we might need to reach out to our greater communities. It takes some courage and energy, but proactively venturing out to seek comforting bonds with new people actually helps build our communities as well as our confidence. Rest assured that there are other like-minded and like-hearted souls out there looking for meaningful connections, especially when their own family members or friends are in crisis or not available.

Here are some ways we can find fellowship with other comforters in nurturing environments:

Volunteering for compassionate or humanitarian programs

Food banks, animal shelters, hospitals, nursing homes, cancer support campaigns, hospices, homeless shelters, elder care and child care services are just a few places we might meet nurturing, like-minded comforters.

Support Groups

Support groups are wonderful venues to meet people in similar situations, who have learned about comforting by going through their own hardship and loss. Caregiver support groups are full of comforters. Group facilitators can also be knowledgeable sources for referrals to programs that provide support and comfort. Further, another benefit for comforters is that caregiver support groups often focus on reinforcing our own self-care and self-comforting practices. It helps to have other comforters root for us to take good care of ourselves.

Our Religious and Spiritual Communities

Finding fellowship through our spiritual interests gets us connected with comforting people on similar paths.

Classes, Study Groups, Clubs, or Events Related
to Topics that Comfort Us

Topics may include spiritual healing, gardening, labyrinths, quilting, networking, massage, pottery, kayaking, bird-watching, and many other enriching activities. (When I moved to Maine nine years ago, I attended a local newcomers club and met a wonderful person who is still one of my best friends.)

Professional Associations and Conferences

A good way to meet comforting colleagues outside of their busy work settings is to attend regular association or networking meetings (often breakfast or luncheon events). The smiling, friendly person at your table who appears comforting might share with you the ways he or she prevents burnout and compassion fatigue.

Self-Comforting Wisdom from Our Guides

Many of the comforting professionals profiled in this book were eager to share the means by which they keep themselves grounded and nurtured. Each of them stressed to me that comfort is as much a vital life support as oxygen, water, or sunlight—it is something that we *all*, comforters and those who are comforted, need to survive. Also, many of them expressed to me a truth I have long observed: The greatest comforters learn by being comfort*ed* by others.

Most of them were regular participants in support groups, twelve-step groups, fitness clubs, or personal development groups. They told me it helped tremendously to have fellow group members rooting for them to take care of themselves. These caregivers and comforters enjoyed being cheered on as they reached their self-care goals.

What grabbed my attention were the striking similarities of the other self-comforting activities practiced by all of our comfort guides. Here are their most popular self-comforting routines.

Quiet Morning Routines

Morning routines involving quietude, reflection, and meditation are vital to all comforters profiled. They take their morning time seriously, as a way to prepare for their comforting work for the day.

Before she goes to work at the Mayo Clinic, Adrienne Dormody enjoys her mornings with her daily comforts.

"I start my day with a cup of hot tea, sitting in my dad's old rocking chair. I begin by reading spiritually uplifting material, including Daily Word and Al-Anon literature and then I pray for those I care deeply about, and for others who are not close to me. Sitting in this chair, I feel held by my father. He died a year after surviving Hurricane Katrina, after barely making it out alive of the 7th Ward (Gentilly area) of New Orleans. In our last months together, when he moved to live with me in Rochester, he enjoyed rocking in this chair that he bought for ten dollars at a local flea market. He was very proud to have purchased it, as he had lost everything in Katrina. Every morning when I rock in his chair, I remember him and feel his spirit."

Patricia Ellen, before arriving at the Center for Grieving Children to direct outreach programs, practices a daily meditation in the morning:

"I start out the day with a meditation practice where I rub my hands together and see myself as a beloved child. I reflect on my need to pace myself and comfort myself. I need to remember to take time to comfort myself, and allow others to comfort me. I admit I have a habit of being more comforting to others than I am to myself. I just cannot take care of everybody. But I am blessed to know wonderful comforting people I can go to as loved ones and colleagues."

Hal Wallof and other comfort guides find comfort in sipping their coffee in the morning and talking intimately with their loved ones. Hal tells us:

"I love to wake up very early and enjoy a cup of coffee while sitting quietly with my wife, slowly transitioning into the day. Once we've had at least one cup of coffee, we talk about each other's dreams—the ones we've had the night before or others. We like to know the details about the good dreams as well as the bad ones, because dreams reveal so much to us about our inner lives. It may seem simple, just drinking coffee and talking about our dreams, but these are some of the most comforting moments we share together."

TAKING LITTLE PAUSES FOR CENTERING, MINDFULNESS, AND PRAYER

Jeff Lewis, a nurse-practitioner at a hectic veterans hospital, believes in the power of taking little pauses throughout his workday, often for only three minutes each. He uses his precious minutes to center himself with prayer.

"When I am in need of comfort, I must first be alone for a while to pray and reflect. I ask myself, 'Is there a lessen I need to learn from this?' Or 'How can I comfort myself today?' Then I take pause and think of my loved ones, alive and deceased."

Alicia Rasin, in her demanding work with the police and with victims of crime, prays frequently throughout the day.

"I spend more time in prayer, and the more I pray, the more I believe God needs me to serve other people in pain. Prayer is a way for me to keep reminding myself what my true purpose is. It's clear to me that I make my prayers real by serving others. Comforting others is my way of being true to God's calling for me. I find comfort in believing God is using me this way, that I have a purpose."

Adrienne shares how she stays centered at her job at the Mayo Clinic:

> "To strengthen myself as a comforter, I've needed to put into practice my centering skills to calm myself. I often need to stop myself when I am getting frustrated, to take a deep breath, step back, and see through the eyes of the patient and their caregivers. I also use centering prayers and the twelve-step Al-Anon teachings to slow myself down and regroup. I definitely have to keep aware of my 'hot buttons,' to honor my limitations and know when to back off and rest. Once again, if I don't take care of myself in this way, the lines of communication are more likely to get crossed and blocked."

READING INSPIRATIONAL
AND ENTERTAINING LITERATURE

All of our comfort guides have favorite books to inspire them, including uplifting memoirs, biographies, poems, short stories, and daily meditations. They frequently read books a second or third time, and study the words closely.

Hal adores Thomas Moore's *Care of the Soul* and other books that beckon him to listen to his soul, as well as gritty, inspirational memoirs. Patricia enjoys the life-affirming poems of Mary Oliver and collects beautiful children's book that are comforting for families. Pam Blunt, an arts therapist, has read Saint-Exupéry's *The Little Prince*

many, many times, and finds joy in reciting Shakespeare's
sonnets.

Adrienne Dormody finds comfort in studying the biblical
story of Job.

"One comforting thing I've discovered recently has surprised me. For the first time, I have been studying the biblical story of Job, and have found this ancient tale speaks to
me about patience and faith. I had fallen into our societal
habit for instant gratification, and had lost the art of wait-
ing, the willingness to wait for things to unfold in their
own time. I certainly have been prone to impatience in
my lifetime, and mythic reminders to have patience are an
important part of my daily rituals of self-comforting."

Amy Handy, a ceramic artist, loves escapist and light
literature for comforting herself. Jennifer Crusie is a favorite author; Amy also happily loses herself listening to audio
books of the Outlander series.

"The ridiculous situations these characters find themselves
in helps me deal with the real curve balls thrown at me
every day. The strange thing is, the whacky stuff in my
favorite books is not as bizarre as what I face every day in
my business. But these stories get me laughing and looking
at my life's dramas in a similar perspective, which lifts me
out of my funk."

Laughing, Playing, and Goofing
Off with Loved Ones and Pets

Jeff Lewis tells us how important it is to just kick back and play with our kids and our pets. He loves to pick up and hold his little loved ones.

> "We've got to make time to play and just be silly. Otherwise, we get in the bad habit of taking ourselves too seriously. I display pictures of my kids and pets playing in my office, to keep me in a lighter mood."

Comfort guides Don and Brenda Weeks, who work with therapy dogs, are in sync with what Jeff says:

> "One of our greatest R&R activities is just watching the goofy stuff dogs do while they are playing. Never a dull moment—great entertainment, and it's free!"

Adrienne Dormody shares her favorite, simple moments of fun with her family:

- Hearing from my son, Allen, and seeing him smile
- Hearing from my brother and nephews
- Hearing my stepson Ryan's laugh
- Laughing at my husband's and my stepson Nathan's jokes

Going to Beautiful Places in Nature

All comfort guides are deeply appreciative of their time in nature. They all walk peacefully in their favorite places, with loved ones and sometimes by themselves. Alicia Rasin loves the James River near her home in Richmond, Virginia, where she goes to restore her spirit.

> "About every other day, I go to the beautiful James River, right here in the busy city of Richmond. I bring my lawn chair, sit down, and watch the waves and the waterfalls along the rocks. Being by water is about as comforting as anything I know."

Pam Blunt adds how she needs her walks:

> "All I need to do is take a walk, even just a short, ten-minute stroll, and I feel better very quickly. The sky is always changing, and the ground is always reflecting back new colors, which reminds me how flowing and resourceful creation around us really is. There is so much supporting us, and when we feel fearful or stuck, we can restore ourselves with a moment of watching the sky or trees or the light on the grass."

GRATITUDE PRACTICES

Simple practices of gratitude, such as keeping a gratitude journal, stopping to say grace before a meal, or posting grateful thoughts online, are commonly enjoyed by our comfort guides.

Les Schaffer, a professional storyteller and former counselor, is a member of a gratitude circle, and shares his post from January 15, 2009. His list of things he appreciates is comforting to read:

Dear Friends:

For today, I am grateful for—

1. All the great posts over the past two days. 2. For your posts reminding me of the friend long ago who taught me that my anxiety attacks were a) not going to kill me, b) under my control, and c) alleviated by talking to people about them. 3. That my back continues to improve, and I'm going to try going to the YMCA for a light workout and some stretching this afternoon. 4. For the fun connections I'm making on Facebook, when it's not crashing my computer. 5. That I did manage to connect with one new friend before my computer crashed today. 6. For the great salmon and squash and asparagus dinner I whipped up last night, despite my back giving me fits. 7. And for the fact that there still is some wild salmon out there, and for the power that created asparagus. 8. How, when I was vegetable gardening, that raising my own asparagus helped teach me patience, sort of like how zucchini teaches us to deal with abundance. 9. That, so far, I am not feeling super-anxious about the busy performing and teaching schedule this winter/spring, even though I do not feel in any way prepared. But things are in progress. 10. Speaking of that, I got invited back to perform at this spring's Arts Festival at the Cultural Arts Center at Glen Allen. 11. For the long johns, flannel shirts, and fleece that enable me to work comfortably in our chilly house—without needing to jack up the thermostat too much. 12. I could not write down enough gratitude for my daughter, whose forty-third birthday is today. It seems like just yesterday she was born, a few ounces short of being a preemie, at the Medical College of Virginia, on a snowy afternoon. When she was born, she could fit in the palm of my hand. Now I fit like putty in her capable hands. 13. That I've survived to be a part of my daughter's life and family.

Later,

Les

KEEPING COMFORTING REMINDERS
AND SOUVENIRS AROUND US

Keeping mementos around us of loved ones, both living and deceased, is a deeply comforting activity. With photos, artwork, cards, quilts, jewelry, and many other special objects, we can keep the loving spirit of our loved ones with us, especially at busy work settings.

Adrienne tells us:

"I often wear my father's watch to work on my left wrist, and my mother's ring on my right hand (she survived Katrina, and continues to live north of New Orleans). With these little treasures, I am reminded of them, and comforted by their spirits. Other keepsakes and photos of my family comfort me both at home and at work."

SHARING MEALS AND GATHERING
WITH FRIENDS AND FAMILY

All of our comfort guides love to make food, share food, and eat food. Sitting down together for a meal with friends and family is certainly on the top ten list of comforting things for everyone.

Alicia smiles to say:

"I love having my friends over to sit on the porch and sip iced tea with some homemade pies. But honestly, going out to dinner with friends is one of my favorite things to do."

Les beams when he talks about his cooking:

"Just putting the dinner I made on the table, and watching people dish it up and pass it around is about as comforting as anything I know."

MUSIC

Music is a must-have for comforters. All the comfort guides told me they listen to music every day, and feel the difference it makes in their energy level and mood. Many of them are quite deliberate about what they listen to before going to see clients and patients as caregivers. Hal listens to Putumayo World Music and still enjoys Simon and Garfunkel. Adrienne never gets tired of hearing Toots and the Maytals and Willie Nelson. Pam Blunt plays Chopin on her piano to clear her mind when she comes home after working with her clients as a psychotherapist. Patricia has a passion for country-western music.

(I have noticed country-western music is full of songs about grief, loss, and abandonment, which can help us release negativity sometimes. When someone has left me high and dry and I feel dissed, I still love the 1977 hit by Kenny Loggins, *You Picked a Fine Time to Leave Me, Lucille*.)

LEARNING ABOUT OTHER PEOPLE IN OTHER REGIONS, CULTURES, AND ERAS

All of the comfort guides also mentioned how important it was for them to learn about perspectives of people from other regions around the United States and from cultures around the world. Many of them enjoyed news and documentaries that shed light on situations in other countries. They said knowledge of what other people on the planet were going through helped them understand better the plight of people in their own communities. In short, a global perspective put local issues into perspective—economic changes, environmental changes, social changes.

Hal says he likes meeting people from other cultures and "finding our commonalities." He also loves to travel and explore.

Alicia adds:

"I really don't see too many movies, and don't watch that much TV, but I do read the news and watch the news on TV. This might sound strange to some people, but I find it comforting to get the news about what other people around the world are going through. When I hear about the people in China or in Africa, or somewhere else, I feel a sense of unity with the whole world, as a part of humanity. This lifts me out of my own little problems and puts things in a bigger perspective. So that's why I think being aware of what's going on around the world is actually very comforting. Sure, you can see a lot of bad stuff going on, but still, there is so much hope out there when you look at the faces of the children in other countries."

Adrienne says she finds comfort in learning new things, as she is a curious person who is genuinely interested in how people live.

"It's comforting for me to learn something stimulating and exciting—a new discovery or a medical cure, or some interesting and inspiring news about how a community is dealing with a problem."

Jeff is a bit of a history buff, and enjoys seeing through the eyes of people from early in the last century, especially through movies. He works with elder veterans and tries to understand their perspective. He watches old movies from the '30s and '40s, including old newsreels. A favorite classic film of his is *The Fighting Sullivans*.

"*The Fighting Sullivans* tells us how to stick together. After all the poor father has lost, including his sons, he stills goes back to work. He finds brotherhood and fatherhood in his caring for his coworkers, his buddies."

GROUNDING, EXERCISE, BODY WORK, AND ENERGY WORK

Energy medicine, yoga, massage, and the martial arts are vital to comforters, especially for those of us prone to losing touch with our body's messages and gut instincts when we push ourselves to serve others. Keeping a routine with these practices helps us read our bodies, know our limits, and honor our energy cycles. To be able to say no is crucial to comforters, but no doesn't mean much if we don't truly heed our body's wisdom about what we can and cannot actually do.

· ❦ ·

Conclusion
Comfort Is All Around Us

ANGELS AT THE DOOR

In the mid-1990s, angels were all the rage. I collected angel cards, angel calendars, angel music, and angel stories, and in my job as a rehab counselor on the oncology unit at a hospital in Richmond, Virginia, angels were my role models for comforting. I also dreamed of the day I would have children to comfort.

Unfortunately, it was during this period that I learned I could never have my own children because of premature ovarian failure. And two months after the day I received this news, on a Friday afternoon in August, I was laid off from my job, along with three hundred others, when the hospital downsized. I felt barren, isolated, and different from other "normal" women I knew. And most of all, I grieved the life I thought I had been destined to live.

That following Saturday, while my husband was away on a long business trip, I cried all day. My angel books and angel music could no longer comfort me. I prayed to God to send me a *real* angel. I was ready for a bona fide spiritual visit from heaven.

The doorbell rang. Oh my God, who could that be? I wondered. It couldn't be an angel, you silly fool, I chided myself. Before I ran downstairs to answer the door, I glanced at myself in the mirror. Pale, puffy, with tear-drenched cheeks, I quickly wiped my face with the bottom of my white polo shirt.

As I approached the door, I checked through the peep hole and saw a small, sweaty, man in a filthy T-shirt and muddy shoes. He must have been one of the laborers who worked on my neighbor's lawn. What was he doing at my door? Annoyed, I almost didn't open the door for him. But I did, and as I stepped onto the porch in the sweltering heat to speak with him, I noticed that a golden retriever was standing next to the man, staring at me, wagging his tail. The man smiled politely and asked, "Is this your dog?"

"No . . ." I answered, drawn to the dog's friendly eyes.

The man struggled to speak in English. "I'm looking for his . . . for his person."

"I'm sorry, but I don't know who he belongs to. I don't have a dog."

The dog panted in the heavy humidity. The man looked upon the dog tenderly and said, "Can he have some . . . some . . ."

"Water? Do you think the dog needs some water?"

"Yeah." He nodded.

"Would *you* like some water?" I asked the man.

"Yeah. Thank you."

"Hold on just a minute." I brought the dog a bowl of water and the man a glass of water. They both stood on my front porch, drinking it down. I realized I was thirsty, too.

The man thanked me again. I asked if there was any more I could do. "Could I call someone about the dog? Would you like some more water?"

"No, that's okay . . . I know somebody who can help me, who has a car and stuff."

"Okay. By the way, you are really nice to be doing this. I hope you find the owner."

He nodded modestly, then left quickly, as the dog followed him eagerly, at ease with the man.

I closed the door and stood in the hallway, stunned. Just ten minutes earlier, desperate enough to go begging to God, I had prayed for a brilliant, glowing angel to come to me. But instead, this humble man and a lost dog had come to my door on this gruelingly hot day. Sure, I could have been suspicious and wary. He might have been using the dog as a cover for something. But no, I felt his good-heartedness and the dog's sweetness and trust instantly. I sauntered to the kitchen, poured myself a glass of water, and drank the coolness down.

Was this stranger my angel? I don't know. But I do know that in witnessing his beautiful kindness toward that dog I was reassured that comforting still existed here on earth even if it didn't in heaven—and this hopeful reminder opened my heart up again. In the end, the art of comforting is nothing more than a language of the heart—someone we barely know or even a complete stranger reaching out to us at just the moment when all hope has left. But how will you know when it is your turn to answer the call? Listen with your heart. And always remember, comfort is all around us. We are never alone.

· ❧ ·

A Little Guidebook *to* Comforting Things

A Guide to Comforting Movies, Books, TV, and Music

Preface to Part Five

THIS FINAL SECTION OF THE BOOK is a handy guide to ideas, suggestions, resources, and practical tips for comforting others. I have divided it into three sections.

SECTION A: COMFORTING FROM THE WORLD OF ENTERTAINMENT: A MEDIA GUIDE

Here are movies, books, music, TV shows, and YouTube videos that people have told me have comforted them. These lists reflect hundreds of individual suggestions derived from sixteen years of facilitating support groups, speaking to audiences, and teaching classes in the art of comforting. I've categorized the media groups into accessible listings and lively genres to make choosing a movie, a book, or music a more enjoyable and comforting experience.

These selections of comforting media listings are only meant to get us started, as samples, not comprehensive, definitive lists. I would not want to have the last word on what comforts us about a movie, a memoir, or a song. I want to inspire comforters to use their imagination and wit in choosing media, and also to use their hearts and intuition in matching media choices to the people we are comforting. The Food Groups for the Soul are presented lightheartedly to help us percolate on ideas for offering comfort to meet the needs of the individual or group.

SECTION B: COMFORTING FROM A TO Z, FROM ANGELS TO ZITHERS

Here's where we can really have fun brainstorming on what's out there in the world to comfort us. These comfort enhancers are listed for us to lighten, soften, and relax the tone of our environments and gatherings. (I admit, I had a blast putting these lists together. And I invite any reader to make their own lists of comforting things.) This exercise in simply writing down the comforting things around us reminds me of the wonderful song "My Favorite Things" from *The Sound of Music*.

Our favorite comforting things are listed in Section B in alphabetical order for easy reference.

SECTION C: COMFORTING RESOURCES AND SUGGESTED READING

This is also a start-up list of comforting websites and suggested reading selections. Once again, I wanted to inspire and stimulate ideas, not to present comprehensive lists. I've chosen in particular websites that have user-friendly, well-organized, pertinent, and updated links, so that these sites serve as clearinghouses and resource guides in their own ways.

· ❦ ·

A Guide to Comforting Things

Section A. Comforting from the World of Entertainment: A Media Guide
Comfort Movies, Comfort Books, Comfort Music

For the past five years, I've gathered lists of suggested comfort movies, books, TV shows, YouTube videos, and music. These reflect the vast input from members of support groups and seminars, dozens of colleagues, and hundreds of audience participants all voicing their most comforting influences from the arts and literature. In collecting this data and finding ways to organize the suggestions, I recognized recurring themes, genres, and styles being recommended, revealing universally comforting works of art. Adding to this, I studied the trends of bestselling books, popular movies, music, and TV shows on Amazon.com, IMDb, Billboard, and many other ratings sites.

I discovered the most important common denominator of a comforting story or song is that it has a good landing with a positive message, giving us hope. Hope and hard work can float us through stormy times—proven in movies, books, and inspirational news clips. A pilot can land a plane on the Hudson, people of color can rise to high positions, slum kids can make it out of the slums, addicts can make it through their recovery. If we are getting jittery that humanity is fast going to hell in a handbasket (economically, environmentally, morally, and militarily), we need to witness a serious spunk in action. Stories and songs sustain us with solid assurance our beloved protagonists are going to succeed somehow, with resource*fulness*, not just resources, coming from inside as much as outside of themselves. This doesn't mean we have to have a "feel good" ending, but at least a "feel better" ending, with characters who triumph over adversity, or muddle through it all pretty well.

For art to be comforting, even if we went through a character's anguish, or a song's yearning, or a painting's intense mood, our spirits are lifted at the end of our encounter. From whimsical to funny to cheery to high-grit inspirational, comfort comes in various nurturing ways for the soul, as long as the take-away vibe is upbeat, either energizing us, calming us, or amusing us. These nurturing variations, themes, and genres have beckoned me to organize them into "food groups" for the soul, because they *feed* the soul. Comforting art can also deal with dark themes, as long as we are reassured at the end that the bad stuff the character or artist went through is well worth the journey.

I have organized six basic "food groups" of comfort for the soul in the arts and media, all containing good landings and hefty doses of positive energy. We are left heartened, comforted, inspired, or at least a bit calmer after our encounter with these creations.

No tragedies are allowed on the following lists, though they are beautiful and important. I know many people say they are comforted by tragedies, but I have found that they are not quite as comforting for most of us, though tragedies are healing in their own ways. Sorry, *Million Dollar Baby*, *Das Boot*, *Mystic River*, *The House of Mirth*, *American Beauty*, *No Country for Old Men*, and so many great movies—not going here! And, of course, horror flicks and extremely violent thrillers are much too rough on the nerves to make the comfort movie lists below. Sorry, *Kill Bill*, *The Exorcist*, *Halloween*, *The Texas Chainsaw Massacre*, *Clockwork Orange*, not going here either.

CLASSIC COMFORT:
FROM HEARTENING TO HILARIOUS

This is comfort we might slip into a "snuggie" to enjoy. Sit back, sip a cup of hot chocolate, and "veg out" when there's no energy left to function. The following classic comforts demand little from us, as no-brainer yet delightful entertainment. We can laugh, coo, sigh, and giggle when we haven't even smiled all day long. When we have a cold or flu and feel yucky overall, this kind of remedy usually works.

Comforting Qualities: Fun, funny, engaging, delightful, cheery, entertaining, reassuring, undemanding, uncomplicated

CLASSIC COMFORT MOVIES AND DVD SETS

Amélie

Anne of Green Gables (DVD boxed sets; with Megan Follows as Anne)

Austin Powers: International Man of Mystery (funny, but might
 be too raunchy for some groups)

Bend It Like Beckham

Best in Show

Blazing Saddles

The Blues Brothers

Breakfast at Tiffany's

Chariots of Fire

Cinema Paradiso

Clueless

Emma

Enchanted April

Ferris Bueller's Day Off

Field of Dreams

Four Weddings and a Funeral

Ghostbusters

Gregory's Girl

Groundhog Day

In Her Shoes

It's a Wonderful Life

Ladies in Lavender

Local Hero

Lost in Translation

Millions

Miss Pettigrew Lives for a Day

My Big Fat Greek Wedding

Persuasion (the 1995 TV series with Amanda Root)

Pollyanna

Pride and Prejudice (the 2005 movie and the 1996 TV series)

A Room with a View

Seabiscuit

The Secret of Roan Inish

Sense and Sensibility

Shirley Temple movies

Sister Act

Sixteen Candles (and other John Hughes films)

Sleepless in Seattle

There's Something About Mary

Under the Tuscan Sun

When Harry Met Sally

The Winter Guest (deals with recovering from grief over loss of a spouse but has a hopeful, heartwarming ending)

CLASSIC COMFORT YOUTUBE VIDEOS

Challenge Day

A Father's Amazing Love

Free Hugs Campaign

Random Acts of Kindness

Stand by Me (Playing for Change)

CLASSIC COMFORT TV SHOWS

Comedy Central Channel, *Jeopardy!*, *Friends*, *Cheers*, *Two Fat Ladies*, *Dog Whisperer*, *The Andy Griffith Show*, *The Carol Burnett Show*, *Mr. Bean*, *Leave It to Beaver*, *Laugh-In*, *The*

Simpsons, Sex and the City, talk shows (such as *Oprah, Ellen, David Letterman*), *Dancing with the Stars, So You Think You Can Dance*

CLASSIC COMFORT MUSIC

Soft rock, light classical (guitar, flute, harp), folk/traditional, light jazz, country-western

SONGS FOR COMFORTING INCLUDE:

"Amazing Grace" (by anyone who sings it)

"Angel" by Sarah McLachlan

"Beautiful" by Christina Aguilera

"Beautiful Day" by U2

"Bridge over Troubled Water" by Simon and Garfunkel

"Calling All Angels" by Jane Siberry with k.d. lang

"Don't Worry, Be Happy" by Bobby McFerrin

"Let It Be" by the Beatles

"Morning Has Broken" by Cat Stevens (Yusuf Islam)

"No Such Thing and Say What You Need to Say" by John Mayer

"Reach Out and Touch (Somebody's Hand)" by Diana Ross

"Shaking the Tree" by Peter Gabriel with Youssou N'Dour

"Smile" by Nat King Cole

"Stand by Me" by Ben E. King

"We Are All Made of Stars" by Moby

"When You Wish Upon a Star" *(sung by Cliff Edwards as character Jiminy Cricket)*

"You've Got a Friend" by James Taylor

Artists:

The Beatles

Donovan

Art Garfunkel

Norah Jones

Nat King Cole

Kenny Loggins

Willie Nelson

Liz Story (light jazz piano—great for dinner parties)

Windham Hill Artists (From jazz to folk to New Age, mostly soft, relaxing)

CLASSIC COMFORT BOOKS (BY TITLE)

Chicken Soup for the Soul series

A Cup of Comfort series

Dewey: The Small-Town Library Cat Who Touched the World by Vicki Myron

Eat, Pray, Love by Elizabeth Gilbert

The Geography of Bliss by Eric Weiner

Gift from the Sea by Anne Morrow Lindbergh

Here If You Need Me by Kate Braestrup

Kitchen Table Wisdom by Rachel Naomi Remen

Living Your Unlived Life: Coping with Unrealized Dreams and Fulfilling Your Purpose in the Second Half of Life by Robert Johnson and Jerry Ruhl

Simple Abundance: A Daybook of Comfort and Joy by Sarah Ban Breathnach

This Place I Know: Poems of Comfort by Georgia Heard (for
children as well as adults, written to address the effects of
9/11, but timeless comfort for any crisis)

FICTION

The Little Prince by Antoine de Saint-Exupery (not just for
children)

Pride and Prejudice by Jane Austen

Under the Tuscan Sun by Francis Mayes

Any humorous work by P. G. Wodehouse

CLASSIC COMFORTING BOOKS PARTICULARLY FOR GRIEF
AND LOSS

A Grief Observed by C. S. Lewis

How to Go On Living When Someone You Love Dies by Therese
Rando

How to Survive the Loss of a Love by Peter McWilliams, Harold
Bloomfield, and Melba Colgrove

Necessary Losses by Judith Viorst

*A Time to Grieve: Meditations for Healing After the Death of a
Loved One* by Carol Staudacher

*Understanding Your Grief: Ten Essential Touchstones for Finding
Hope and Healing Your Heart* by Alan Wolfelt

When Bad Things Happen to Good People by Rabbi Harold
Kushner

CLASSIC COMFORT LISTS FOR CHILDREN
Comfort Movies for Children

For a helpful guide to choosing movies for children and families, I recommend the book *The Best Old Movies for Families: A Guide to Watching Together* by Ty Burr.

Also, checking in with *Movie Mom* (Nell Minow) on the *Belief Net* website, parents are given good guidance to what's comforting and appropriate (or not) with new releases for children and teens. Nell also compiles innovative theme lists of movie recommendations to help families pick the right flicks.

According to hundreds of people I've asked, one of the most all-time comforting movies for families and children is *Finding Nemo*. More recently, dozens of people have told me the tender story of the movie *Up* has been comforting, too, dealing with loss issues. There is a great moment in the *Up* story, when a little boy says he misses a loved one, not because of the exciting things they did together, but because of the "boring" everyday things they shared together. I find this to be true about the comforting times in our lives, as we enjoy the ordinary routines and simple pastimes of daily life more than we might realize.

HERE ARE SOME POPULAR COMFORTING FAVORITES:

Finding Nemo

Harry Potter series

The Incredibles

The Lion King (Disney 2003 Platinum DVD edition)

Mary Poppins (with Julie Andrews and Dick Van Dyke)

The Music Man (1962)

Shirley Temple movies

WALL-E

Willy Wonka and the Chocolate Factory (1971)

Up

CLASSIC COMFORT BOOKS FOR CHILDREN (AGES 1 TO 3)

Boynton's Greatest Hits (both Volume I and Volume II)
   by Sandra Boynton

Brown Bear, Brown Bear, What Do You See? by Bill Martin Jr.

Goodnight, Moon by Margaret Wise Brown

Pat the Bunny by Dorothy Kunhardt

Peek-a-Who? by Nina Laden

Snuggle Puppy (Boynton on Board) by Sandra Boynton

CLASSIC COMFORT BOOKS FOR CHILDREN (AGES 4 TO 8)

Alexander and the Terrible, Horrible, No Good, Very Bad Day
   by Judith Viorst

A Child's Garden of Verses by Robert Louis Stevenson

Clifford's First Snow Day by Norman Bridwell

Frog and Toad Are Friends by Arnold Lobel

George and Martha by James Marshall

Guess How Much I Love You by Sam McBratney

A Hatful of Seuss by Dr. Seuss

Mike Mulligan and His Steam Shovel by Virginia Lee
   Burton

Millions of Cats by Wanda Gag

The Nutshell Library by Maurice Sendak

Olivia by Ian Falconer

Owl Moon by Jane Yolen

The Tales of Peter Rabbit by Beatrix Potter

The Tenth Good Thing About Barney by Judith Viorst

The Velveteen Rabbit by Margery Williams Bianco

CLASSIC COMFORT BOOKS FOR CHILDREN (AGES 9 TO 12)

The Book of Three by Lloyd Alexander

Charlotte's Web by E. B. White

Chitty Chitty Bang Bang by Ian Fleming

The Complete Tales and Poems of Winnie-the-Pooh by A. A. Milne

The Lion, the Witch and the Wardrobe by C. S. Lewis

Mary Poppins by P. L. Travers

M. C. Higgins, the Great by Virginia Hamilton

The Princess and the Goblin by George McDonald

The Secret Garden by Frances Hodgson Burnett

See You Around, Sam! by Lois Lowry

A Wrinkle in Time by Madeleine L'Engle

COMFORTING BOOKS FOR CHILDREN DEALING WITH THE
DEATH OF A LOVED ONE (RECOMMENDED BY COMFORT
GUIDE PATRICIA ELLEN, OUTREACH DIRECTOR OF THE
CENTER FOR GRIEVING CHILDREN IN PORTLAND, MAINE)

Lifetimes: Healing for Children and Adults by Bryan Mellonie
    (for ages 3 to 6)

The Next Place by Warren Hanson (for ages 6 to adult)

Thank You, Grandpa by Lynne Plourde (for ages 4 to 8)

When Dinosaurs Die: A Guide to Understanding Death by Laurie
  Krasny Brown (for ages 4 to 8)

RECOMMENDED BY OTHER COMFORT GUIDES
FOR CHILDREN DEALING WITH LOSS

Badger's Parting Words by Susan Varley (for ages 4 to 8)

The Fall of Freddie the Leaf: A Story of Life for All Ages by Leo
  Buscaglia (for ages 4 to 8, or older)

Fig Pudding by Ralph Fletcher (for ages 9 to 12)

*Help Me Say Goodbye: Activities for Helping Kids Cope When a
  Special Person Dies* by Janis Silverman (for ages 4 to 9)

*I Wish I Could Hold Your Hand: A Child's Guide to Grief and
  Loss* by Pat Palmer (for ages 9 to 12)

Sad Isn't Bad: A Good-Grief Guidebook for Kids Dealing with Loss
  by Michaelene Mundy (for ages 4 to 8)

Tear Soup by Pat Schwiebert (for ages 4 to 8)

There's a Nightmare in My Closet by Mercer Mayer (for ages
  4 to 8)

*Water Bugs and Dragonflies: Explaining Death to Young Children
  (Looking Up)* by Doris Stickney (ages 4 to 9)

CLASSIC COMFORT MUSIC FOR CHILDREN

Baby's Bedtime (sung by Judy Collins and Ernest Troost)
  (for ages 0 to 2)

The Celtic Lullaby (for ages 2 to 5)

Dreamland: World Lullabies and Soothing Songs (for ages
  newborn to 10, or older)

For Our Children: 10th Anniversary Edition (for ages 3 to 9)

For Our Children Too! (for ages 3 to 9)

Lullaby: A Collection (various artists) (for ages 1 to 6)

On a Starry Night (various artists) (ages 2 to 6)

Raffi's music, any of his albums with songs for children

Really Rosie by Carole King

Return to Pooh Corner (sung by Kenny Loggins) (all ages, 1 to adult)

Sesame Street Platinum: All-Time Favorites (for ages 3 to 6)

Songs from a Parent to a Child (sung by Art Garfunkel)

Walt Disney Records–Song Albums: Children's Favorite Songs (for ages 3 to 9)

World Playground (Putumayo World Music Series) (for ages 1 to 10, or older)

GRITTY COMFORT: TRIUMPH OVER ADVERSITY

Themes: true grit, underdogs, coming of age, recovery and healing, rags to riches, victory tales, the attainment of wisdom, stories of courage and moral strength, comeback stories, and bio pics. When we have plenty of energy but feel frustrated, wickedly cynical, or anxious, we might snap out of our funk with something from the more demanding, grittier menu of comforts. The endings in these movies may not be classically "feel-good," but they are hopeful, "feel-better" endings, conveying the strength, resilience, and resourcefulness of the lead characters facing bleak situations. These tougher, riveting stories often can be ultimately comforting for us to boost our belief in the power of the human spirit.

Comforting qualities: gutsy, hopeful, inspirational, life-affirming, spunky.

GRITTY COMFORT MOVIE LIST

An Angel at My Table

Antwone Fisher

Apollo 13

Billy Elliot

The Color Purple

Dreamgirls

Erin Brockovich

Good Will Hunting

Hope and Glory

In America

The Kite Runner

Michael Clayton

Milk

The Miracle Worker (1962, with Patty Duke)

My Life as a Dog

The Pianist

Places in the Heart

Ray

Rocky

The Shawshank Redemption

Slumdog Millionaire

Waitress

Walk the Line

MUSIC

Sound tracks (from the movies listed above),
Motown, Upbeat Rock, Rap and Hip Hop, R&B,
Jazz, Funk

TV SHOWS

The Closer, Prime Suspect, Grey's Anatomy

YOUTUBE VIDEOS

Bernard LaChance's Video for Oprah

Jason McElway's Basketball Game

Randy Pausch's last lecture: *Achieving Your Childhood Dreams*

BOOKS

Inspirational Biographies

Dare to Dream!: 25 Extraordinary Lives by Sandra McCleod
Humphrey

101 World Heroes by Simon Montefiore

Inspirational Memoirs and Other Nonfiction

Angela's Ashes by Frank McCourt

Breakfast at Sally's: One Homeless Man's Inspirational Journey
by Richard LeMieux

Bridge Across My Sorrows by Christina Noble and
Robert Coram

This Child Will Be Great by Ellen Johnson Sirleaf, President
of Liberia

The Heart of a Woman by Maya Angelou

Invictus: Nelson Mandela and the Game That Made a Nation
   by John Carlin

Man's Search for Meaning by Viktor E. Frankl

My Left Foot by Christy Brown

Nothing Is Impossible: Reflections on a New Life and *Still Me*
   by Christopher Reeve

The Story of My Life by Helen Keller

Three Cups of Tea by Greg Mortenson

Fiction

Beloved by Toni Morrison

The Color Purple by Alice Walker

Works by Charles Dickens

Q and A by Vikas Swarup

QUIRKY COMFORT:
SCREWED-UP BUT LOVABLE PEOPLE
MUDDLING THROUGH

Quirky, endearing indies we adore. Keeping the "fun" in dysfunctional families, communities, and love interests. Road trips, offbeat coming of age, funky problem-solving. Forget trying to be "normal."

Comforting Qualities: Humility, accepting our imperfection, compassion, resourcefulness, wit, humor.

QUIRKY COMFORT MOVIES

About a Boy

As Good As It Gets

Being There

Big Night

Finding Normal

(500) Days of Summer

The Full Monty

Garden State

In Good Company

Juno

Lars and the Real Girl

Little Miss Sunshine

My Dinner with André

Raising Arizona

The Royal Tenenbaums

Sideways

That Thing You Do!

Tootsie

The Wild Parrots of Telegraph Hill

You Can Count on Me

Young at Heart

YOUTUBE

Funny cat videos (lots of these)—there are so many good ones
   that I couldn't pick a favorite

London–10 Quirky Places

TV SHOWS

Almost anything by Jeanne Moos on CNN

*House, Monk, 30 Rock, Frasier, Seinfeld, Desperate Housewives,
   Sex and the City, Glee*

BOOKS

Chic lit books by Jennifer Crusie

In Her Shoes by Jennifer Weiner

One for the Money by Janet Evanovich (a Stephanie Plum
novel)

MUSIC

Alvin and the Chipmunks

Beastie Boys

Björk

Garden State sound track

Katy Perry

Lady Gaga

The Pussycat Dolls

Tiptoe Through the Tulips (sung by Tiny Tim)

Walk Like an Egyptian (The Bangles)

ESCAPIST COMFORT: TO GET WAY, WAY OUT OF DODGE

Willingly ejecting ourselves off our couches to other planets, other dimensions, other worlds, and spiraling through time travel. Categories include fantasy, sci-fi, time travel, animation . . . Bollywood?

Comforting Qualities: Imaginative, absorbing, highly immersive, colorful, different, exotic, "out there."

Escapist Comfort Movies

Avatar

Babe

Back to the Future

Big Fish

Chronicles of Narnia: The Lion, the Witch and the Wardrobe

The Curious Case of Benjamin Button

Disney fairy tales and other tales (*Peter Pan, Sleeping Beauty,*
    Cinderella, The Little Mermaid, Pinocchio)

Enchanted

E.T.

Fantasia

The Fifth Element

Finding Nemo

Harry Potter (all)

The Incredibles

Indiana Jones movies

The Lion King

Mad Max

Pleasantville

The Princess Bride

Spirited Away

Star Trek

Star Wars

WALL-E

The Wiz

The Wizard of Oz

TV
Syfy (Sci-Fi Channel)

BOOKS
The Chronicles of Narnia by C. S. Lewis
The Crystal Cave (Mary Stewart's Merlin Trilogy)
Grimm Fairy Tales
Lord of the Rings Trilogy by J. R. R. Tolkien
Outlander series by Diana Gabaldon
The Sword and the Stone by T. H. White

MUSIC
"Afternoon of a Faun" by Claude Debussy
The Best of Vangelis
Mad Max sound track
"Mother Goose Suite" (Maurice Ravel)
Music from the Cosmos series with Carl Sagan
Music of Delerium
Music of the Moody Blues: *Days of Future Passed, Every Boy
Deserves Favour* albums
Music of A. R. Rahman
Oxygène (Jean-Michel Jarre—early electronica but still a
classic)
The Science Fiction Album (collection)
Sound tracks from Disney, fantasy, and sci-fi movies
Stargate music tracks
Star Wars sound track

MUSICAL COMFORT: SONGS GALORE
FOR ANY OCCASION

Musicals and sound tracks full of tunes, to match our many moods, wishes, and whims.

MUSICAL COMFORT MOVIES

Camelot

Funny Girl

Grease

Hairspray

Hello, Dolly!

Mamma Mia!

Mary Poppins

The Music Man

The Rocky Horror Picture Show (a cult classic, quite raunchy but very entertaining)

Seven Brides for Seven Brothers

Singing in the Rain

The Sound of Music

Willy Wonka and the Chocolate Factory (with Gene Wilder)

MUSIC

Sound tracks for musical movies

SUBLIME COMFORT: HEAVEN ON EARTH

Comfort expressed spiritually, joyously, or gently, bringing a sense of grace into art, such as the angelic voice of someone singing "Ave Maria," or the image of an eagle in flight.

These moments give us chills, touching what is sacred inside our souls.

Comforting Qualities: Spiritual, soulful, awe-inspiring, serene, elegant.

FILMS/DVDS

Celtic Woman (DVDs of the singers of the series)

Chronos

Earth

Joseph Campbell and the Power of Myth (Bill Moyers DVDs)

Riverdance

Winged Migration

MUSIC (BY ARTIST OR GROUP)

Anonymous 4 (albums: *American Angels: Songs of Hope, Redemption & Glory*, and *An English Ladymass: Medieval Chant and Polyphony*)

Anuna, an Irish choir famous for the music of *Riverdance*

Bach, "Joy of Man's Desiring"

Sarah Brightman, an English singer with an angelic voice (albums: *La Luna* and *Eden*)

Bill Douglas (album: *Deep Peace*)

Celtic Woman: all angelic voices

Enya, an Irish singer famous for *Orinoco Flow* (album: *The Best of Enya*)

James Galway (album: *Meditations: Serenely Beautiful Flute Music by James Galway*)

Gluck, *Orpheus and Eurydice* (*Dance of the Blessed Spirits*)

Bobby McFerrin (album: *Simple Pleasures* with hit single
 "Don't Worry, Be Happy")

Loreena McKennitt

Pachelbel, *Canon in D Major*

Franz Schubert, "Ave Maria"

Joanne Shenandoah, a Native American singer, musician,
 and composer (album: *Peace and Power: The Best of Joanne
 Shenandoah*)

Hildegard von Bingen (album: *Hildegard von Bingen: Canticles
 of Ecstasy*)

Vaughn Williams, *Fantasia on a Theme by Thomas Tallis*

Yanni, a Greek musician and composer

BOOKS

Anam Cara by John O'Donohue

Anything by Maya Angelou

The Art of Being: 101 Ways to Practice Purpose in Your Life
 by Dennis Merritt Jones

*The Art of Happiness, 10th Anniversary Edition: A Handbook
 for Living* by the Dalai Lama and Howard Cutler

The Artist's Way by Julia Cameron

Care of the Soul by Thomas Moore

Enduring Grace: Living Portraits of Seven Women Mystics
 by Carol L. Flinders

Heart Steps by Julia Cameron

Myths to Live By by Joseph Campbell

A New Earth by Eckhart Tolle

A Pocketful of Miracles by Joan Borysenko

Poetry by Mary Oliver

Poetry by Robert Bly

Poetry by Rumi

The Prophet by Kahlil Gibran

When Things Fall Apart by Pema Chodron

Women in Praise of the Sacred: 43 Centuries of Spiritual Poetry by Women (Edited by Jane Hirshfield)

And great spiritual teachings in the religious texts of all cultures.

· ❧❀ ·

Section B. Comforting from A to Z, from Angels to Zithers

Activities and Enhancers for Creating a Comforting Atmosphere

We can add the following ingredients to our homes for creating a comforting atmosphere with our families and friends.

But first, before we go down the A to Z list, here are the top fifteen comforting essentials, the all-time favorite things most people need for comfort (not in any order).

THE TOP FIFTEEN COMFORTING ESSENTIALS

The Arts for expressing ourselves, especially when words are hard to find

Belief, a sense of meaning or purpose

Comfort foods and drinks

A comfortable place, home, or sanctuary, a sheltered, safe place to rest and restore oneself

Connection, a sense of belonging, community, being relational, having a support system

Entertainment, media, games (including mindless distractions)

Gratitude, recognizing what supports us

Humor

Interests, passions, hobbies, outlets

Love, affection, warmth

Medication/treatment/therapy

Nature, being connected with the Earth

Pets, animals

Sports

Touch, caresses, hugs, massages, footbaths, brushing hair, putting on lotion, putting on nail polish or makeup, sexual contact

And a little factoid: In times of economic hardship, people spend money on chocolate, lipstick, movies, and games more than most commodities. I hear sewing kits, craft-making kits, and Snuggie sales are going pretty well, too.

AND HERE IS MY WHOLE LIST OF LIFE'S COMFORTS.

A

Angels, images of, music inspired by

Animals (our beloved pets, companion animals, pet toys, cartoon animals, Animal Planet)

Antiques

Apples, apple cider, apple pie, applesauce

Aquariums

Arbors

Aromatherapy (especially lavender and chamomile)

Art

Atriums

B

Banana splits

Baskets, full of little things (candies, stones, flowers, goofy toys)

Baths (bubble baths, mineral baths)

Biographies, books, shows, biography movies

Birds, bird-watching, bird feeders, bird sounds

Blankets and throws

Blessings

Bluebirds

Blue jeans

Boats, toy boats

Bread

Brushing hair slowly with a soft brush

Bubble baths

Bubble gum

Bubbles, bubble-making toys

C

Candles

Card games

Cards, greeting cards, sympathy cards

Cartoons

Cedar chests

Chicken soup

Chocolate, hot chocolate

Cider

Cinnamon, cinnamon rolls

Clay

Coffee

Comedies

Comforters

Comic books, comics

Compassion
Cookies
Cotton clothing
Crackers, cheese and crackers.
Crafts
Crayons
Crossword puzzles
Curios
Curry

D

Distractions, pleasant or
    mindless
Dogs
Dollops . . . of sour cream . . .
Doodling
Doughnuts
Doves
Dried flowers
Dr. Seuss children's books
Ducks, including rubber
    duckies for the tub

E

Earl Grey tea
Eggnog
Egg rolls
Eloise books (not only for kids)
Empathy
Enchiladas
Entertainment
Eucalyptus
Exuberance

F

Facials
Feathers

Ferns
Finger food
Fireplaces, campfires
Fish and chips
Flannel sheets and pajamas
Flowers
Folk dancing, folk music
Footbaths and foot massages
Footsie (appropriately playing it
    under the table)
Fountains
Fruit
Fudge

G

Gardens
Gifts, thoughtful or funky
Gnomes
Golf
Grace
Graham crackers
Grandfather clocks
Grandfathers and grandmothers
Gratitude

H

Harps
Herbs, herbal teas,
    herb gardens
Honey
Hope
Hot-water bottles
House-decorating magazines
    and TV shows
Hugs
Hula hoops
Humor

Hydrangeas
Hymns

I
Ice cream
Indian summer
Inns
Irises
Italian food

J
Jams and jellies
Jazz, light jazz
Jell-O
Jigs
Jigsaw puzzles
Jiminy Cricket
Jokes

K
Kaleidoscopes
Karaoke
Keepsakes
Key lime pie
Kisses, real ones, and also
    Hershey's Kisses
Kitchen tables
Kites
Kittens
Knickknacks
Knitting

L
Lasagna
Laughter
Letters

Lilies
Lilts
Lipstick
Lollipops
Looney Tunes cartoons
Lotions
Lounge chairs
Love
Love seats
Luck

M
Magic kits for kids
Manicures
Marshmallows (roasted, too)
Mashed potatoes
Meat loaf
Milk
Mints (chocolate mints, too)
Money (a little here and there,
    and placed inside cards)
Monopoly (the game)
Motown
Movies/media (see media lists
    in Section A)
Muffins
Music (see media lists in
    Section A)
Music boxes
Musk

N
Nachos
Nail polish
National Enquirer (absurdly
    funny articles and photos)

Night-lights

Nirvana

Notebooks, note cards

Novels, light reading, heart-warming stories (see media lists in Section A)

Nuts—peanuts, cashews, almonds

O

Omelets

Oprah

Oreo cookies

Origami

Orzo pasta

Oscars (watching the show and red carpet glitz)

Oz

Ozzie and Harriet

P

Panache

Pancakes

Pansies

Parsley

Parties

Pastorale

Pat-a-cake game for children

Peace

Pearls, also pearls of wisdom

Penguins

Peppermint (gum, lotion, tea)

Peter Pan

Photographs

Picnics

Pies

Piggy banks

Pigtails

Pillows

Pine cones

Ping-Pong games

Pizza

Post-it notes (they comfort your memory)

Pot roast

Praise

Prayers

Prizes (for all occasions)

Pubs

Pudding

Pumpkins

Puppies

Q

Quarters (for parking meters and such)

Quartz crystals

Queen Anne's lace

Quiet

Quilts

Quiz shows

R

Radios

Rainbows

Recess

Recipes

Reflexology for sore feet

Reindeer

Restaurants

Rewards

Ricotta cheese

Rings
Rituals
Rivers
Robes
Roller skating
Rooms with a view
Roses

S
Sage
Sailing
Salves
Sand (sand trays,
  sandboxes, and sandy
  beaches)
Saxophones
Scones
Scrabble
Seashells
Sex
Shopping
Shrines
Silk
Skates
Skylights
Sliding boards
Smiles
Snoozing
Snuggies
Soaps
Soul
Spaghetti
Sparrows
Spunk
Storybooks
Sunflowers
Sunshine

Sweeties
Swings
Sympathy cards
Syrup

T
Taffy
Talismans
Tambourines
Tandoori chicken
Tapioca pudding
Teapots
Teddy bears
Teletubbies
Thoughtfulness
Tic Tacs
Tinkerbell
Tips
Toffee
Torches
Totems
Toys
Trees
Troll dolls
Tulips
Twitter

U
Umbrellas
Unhurried
Unicorns
Unity

V
Validation
Value

Velcro
Venus
Vermouth
Videos
Vineyards
Violins
Volleyball

W
Waffles
Wagging dog tails
Walks
Waltzes
Warmth from people
Water
Whipped cream
Whistles
Whoopie cushions
Whoopie pies
Wildflowers
Wings
Wisdom
Wishes
Wit

Wonder
Wonton soup
Wood-burning stoves
Wreaths

X
XXX's
Xylophones

Y
Yarn
Yellow
Yes
Yoga
Yo-yos
YouTube (some of the videos, not all)
Yucca plants

Z
Zen
Zest
Zigzags
Zithers

· ❦ ·

Section C. Comforting Resources and Suggested Reading
RESOURCES: COMFORTING WEBSITES
Comforting Gifts to Give and Share

- The Comfort Company
  www.thecomfortcompany.net

Comforting gifts for remembrance, such as memorial ornaments, sympathy cards and gifts, personalized objects and jewelry, keepsakes, art and prints, angels, all kinds of comforts for grieving people. Also a good resource list for other gifts, such as gift baskets. (Oprah has recognized and praised the company's owner, Renee Wood, a former social worker.)

Comforting Books, Games, Activities, and Media for Children

- Parents' Choice Foundation, Parents' Choice Awards

  www.Parents-choice.org

  Diana Huss Green, founder of Parents' Choice, gathers parents, educators, librarians, and other critics to review books, toys, games, and media for children. Diana has written articles about comfort books, such as "Finding Comfort in a Book," on other sites such as www.education.com. Diana has created criteria for comfort books for children emphasizing stories with solid moral values and kindhearted characters. Her comfort book lists are wonderful and carefully selected.

- Children's books on About.com

  childrensbooks.about.com

  Plenty of guidance on books for children ages zero to twelve. I especially like the attention to little ones under six years of age, with great information on colorful picture books for reading aloud. Contains creative categories for selecting books, with a blog and helpful newsletter.

- Education.com: Bringing Learning to Life
  www.education.com

  Aimed at parents, full of great ideas for activities, reading, games, and learning experiences with their children. This site helps families think of home-based activities.

Comforting Inspiration

- Belief Net
  www.beliefnet.com

  For all kinds of spiritual seeker, this entertaining and informative site has something for everyone, for all religions and spiritual traditions. There are lists of comfort movies and books, and other comforts such as blessings, prayers, quotes, personal essays and stories, and plenty of inspirational news about what people around the world are doing to comfort others.

- Simple Abundance
  www.simpleabundance.com

  Sarah Ban Breathnach's wonderful book *Simple Abundance: A Daybook of Comfort and Joy* was the beginning of a series of highly comforting writings. Her website is loaded with current comforting news, articles, and resources for calming and quieting ourselves.

Caregiver Support

- Family Caregiving 101
  www.familycaregiving101.org

Helpful, basic, practical education and support for caregivers. A great primer.

- National Family Caregivers Association
  www.nfcacares.org

  Now on Twitter and building e-communities and family caregiver forums, this site is highly useful for busy caregivers.

- AARP, Family Caregiving
  www.aarp.org/family/caregiving

  AARP has excellent guidance and support for caregivers in their fifties and older.

Grief and Bereavement

- HelpGuide.org

  HelpGuide's Helping a Grieving Person: www.helpguide .org/mental/helping_grieving.htm

  Solid, well-rounded guidance on offering comfort and support for grieving people. Has special sections for supporting adults, as well as grieving teens and children. Links to superior articles and resources.

- MentalHelp.net
  www.mentalhelp.net

  A vast and comprehensive site for a wide range of mental health issues, and includes excellent pages for guidance on the grief process as well as for supporting grieving adults and children.

- The Center for Loss and Life Transition and Companion Press Bookstore
  www.centerforloss.com

Psychiatrist Alan Wolfelt offers a comforting program of "companioning" with grieving people, and his helpful, accessible books are available at his Companion Press Bookstore online.

- Beyond Indigo
  www.beyondindigo.com

  Lots of online support for all kinds of grief, with great places for posting and connecting our thoughts, feelings, and remembrances.

- AARP, Life After Loss
  www.aarp.org/family/lifeafterloss

  Full of helpful and practical articles for bereaved families, and also support for coping with issues related to aging.

- GriefNet
  www.griefnet.org

  The virtual memorial program is comforting, with plenty of online support groups that can be joined for a small fee.

- Hospice Foundation of America, Grief and Loss Support
  www.hospicefoundation.org/griefandloss

  Recommended reading: "Shattering the 8 Myths of Grieving" and "8 Myths About Children and Loss." Great articles and links for all kinds of bereavement issues, as well as caregiver and end-of-life issues. Also, the popular *Journeys* newsletter for bereaved families is available here.

For Bereaved Families Who Have Lost Children

- The Compassionate Friends
  www.compassionatefriends.org

Grieving Children and Teens

- The Dougy Center

  www.dougy.org

  One of the oldest and most highly respected centers for grieving children and teens. This inspirational program is a popular and successful model for many centers nationwide. They have a great online store for books to help grieving children and teens, as well as a search engine for finding grief support resources in your city or state.

Pet Loss

- HelpGuide's Pet Loss Support

  www.helpguide.org/mental/grieving_pets.htm#online

  A good starting place for coping with the death of a pet.

End-of-Life Issues

- Growth House

  www.growthhouse.org

  For issues related to end-of-life matters, caring for a dying loved one, providing support and comfort, as well as facing grief and anticipatory grief.

- Hospice Foundation of America

  www.hospicefoundation.org

  Highly comprehensive, used by professionals in hospice and palliative care and by family caregivers alike.

For Endings of Relationships and Divorce

- Getting Past Your Past

  www.gettingpastyourpast.wordpress.com

- Getting Past Your Breakup
  www.gettingpastyourbreakup.com
    Susan Elliott, a former grief counselor and lawyer, has created an inspirational and informative website and book of the same name to help us through breakups of all kinds.
- Divorce Support
  www.divorcesupport.com
    A well-established, well-used site, very interactive with blogs and forums; full of topics dealing with divorce.
- MentalHelp.net
  www.mentalhelp.net
    On this vast site, the topic of divorce is well covered, from getting through it to recovering from it. Good search program for locating local therapists, and recommendations for current books and articles.

Comforting for Loss of a Job

- Riley Guide, Coping with Job Loss
  www.rileyguide.com/cope.html
    The section of the Riley Guide offers both practical and emotional guidance and links to online support groups, resources, and networks.
- Career Planning at About.com and Job Searching at About.com
  http://careerplanning.about.com
    Dawn Rosenberg McKay addresses job loss, job transition, and unemployment issues on her extensive Career Change pages.

For more practical and detailed information on doing a job search, About.com guide Alison Doyle is helpful with her Job Search pages and has a busy blog (http://jobsearch .about.com). I have used these guides over the years in my social work tasks, helping clients coping with job loss and financial losses, and have found them to be highly reliable and consistently updated.

For Coping with Trauma and PTSD

- Gift from Within
  www.giftfromwithin.org

  This is an international organization to help survivors of trauma and victimization. It's comprehensive and well organized, with informative and encouraging articles, guidance, and resources. It is also helpful for those who care for traumatized individuals. Excellent for locating support groups, Web casts, and many other online supports.
- MentalHelp.net
  www.mentalhelp.net

  Excellent guidance for trauma support, as well as for coping with disasters, violence, and abuse and dealing with other kinds of anxiety.

Connecting to the Disability Community

Here are two essential websites for resources on disabilities:

- Wounded Warrior Project
  www.woundedwarriorproject.org

- Disability.gov
  www.disability.org

Comforting and Healing with the Arts

- Arts and Healing Network
  www.artheals.org

  This network has fantastic links to organizations and healing artists around the world. It's very comprehensive, well organized, and inspirational. Go exploring on this site and your spirit will get a boost. Check out the Image Quilt—beautiful and comforting.

- Paint Your Own Pottery
  www.paintyourownpottery.net

  A site to help your family find a place to paint pottery near you, anywhere in the United States.

- The Foundation for Hospital Art
  www.hospitalart.com

  A program providing volunteers for painting artwork and murals and decorating hospitals to create a comforting atmosphere.

- Now I Lay Me Down to Sleep
  www.nowilaymedowntosleep.org

  This is an organization that provides photographers (at no charge) to take pictures of families in hospitals, when an infant is very ill and not likely to live. The photographer will come to the hospital and take pictures of the infant in the arms of the parents and with the family.

- Project Compassion

  www.heropaintings.com/kzindex.aspx

  This is an organization that helps grieving families dealing with the loss of a loved one who gave his or her life in service to the armed forces. An artist will paint a portrait of the deceased veteran to commemorate the service and comfort the family.

- Playing for Change

  www.playingforchange.com

  They produced and organized the highly popular *Stand By Me* on YouTube, as musicians around the world gather in the name of peace.

Comforting with Nature and Connecting with the Earth

- Roots and Shoots

  www.rootsandshoots.org

  This international program developed by Jane Goodall teaches children and families about taking care of our earth, in our own communities and around the world. Many schools and nature centers have adopted this highly popular program throughout the United States.

Three Great Books about Comforting Others

The Etiquette of Illness: What to Say When You Can't Find the

Words by Susan P. Halpern

This is highly recommended reading for supporting people who are dealing with severe and life-threatening illness.

Healing Conversations: What to Say When You Don't Know What to Say by Nance Guilmartin

Not just for bereavement, this book covers many difficult and challenging times in our lives (loss of job, divorce, illness, crisis), and offers guidance for what to say to those in the midst of these times.

Turning to One Another: Simple Conversations to Restore Hope to the Future by Margaret J. Wheatley

This book is gently written yet deeply inspiring for restoring the art of fostering good conversation, in both home and work settings.

Books for Comforting Ourselves

The Book of Comforts: Simple, Powerful Ways to Comfort Your Spirit, Body and Soul by Patricia Alexander and Michael Burgos

Chicken Soup for the Soul series

Cup of Comfort series

Sites of Our Contributing Comfort Guides

Amy Handy's Clay Play Site
www.clay-play.com

Patricia Ellen at the Center for Grieving Children
www.cgcmaine.org

Les Schaffer at the Tell Tale Hearts Storytellers Theater
www.telltalehearts.org

Nancy Coyne's site
www.heartsworknancycoyne.com

The Epona Center
www.taoofequus.com

Jen Deraspe's Nurture Through Nature Retreat Center
www.ntnretreats.com

Acknowledgments:
The Return of the Blue Herons

Finally the Maine landscape, once white, then gray, then muddy, has turned a brilliant green this spring. Lilacs, irises, and apple blossoms burst forth along the sidewalks of the town of Yarmouth. It has been a rougher than usual winter, even for Mainers, and now people glow in their relief and pleasure. Everyone moves with a spring in their step, young fathers and mothers pushing baby strollers, older couples with dogs, packs of teens running in track clothes, and kids charging ahead on their bicycles.

But, as tranquil as my little town of Yarmouth is this afternoon, the promise of a beautiful evening beckons me to return to Wolfe's Neck Woods for a walk in the long light through the pines. This evening I yearn especially to see the great blue herons. I have not seen a single heron since November, for six cold months. I know they love Wolfe's Neck Woods, where the Harraseeket River meets the wide Casco Bay, beside Googins Island. A heron colony thrives nearby, on another tiny island, one of the largest refuges for herons in New England, protected by the state of Maine and the Nature Conservancy.

I arrive at the rocks near Googins Island, where the ospreys are busy as usual. I step easily along the large flat rocks of the shoreline to a small sandy beach and sit on a patch of moss. Though the tide is low and the glistening, spongy bottom of the sea is exposed and bustling with birdlife, I see no herons. Odd, I think. Herons are usually here, standing in clusters, very still, like sentinels, watching quietly for fish.

This is a time to be still. I decide to stop watching for the herons to arrive, and lie down on the warm sand, gazing upon the tall grasses swaying in the moist sea breezes, breathing in the clean, sweet scents of bayberry and pine. Lulled by the slow-lapping waves, I rest my eyes on the silver blue light of the rising crescent moon. I settle into a glowing sense of gratitude, remembering the immense generosity of all my comforting colleagues who have offered me their insights as well as their stories. One by one, I picture their kind faces and hear echoes of their voices. I adore each one of them and marvel at their wisdom.

A gust of wind grabs my attention and sprays a few tiny drops of the sea on my face. I sit up. I take off my shoes and step slowly into the cool, frothy water at the edge of the bay. So moved, and bursting with joy and gratitude, I begin to speak out loud my thanks to my comforting colleagues, friends, family, animals, and more. I speak in reverence for the providence of all my comforters.

First, I thank my comfort guides for what they have

taught me, and for the distinct comforting qualities of their true natures:

Jeff, for his gift of deeply appreciating and respecting his patients as a nurse.

Adrienne, for her integrity, humility, and wisdom in helping us communicate difficult things with our providers as well as our loved ones.

Alicia, for teaching us to be real, to be ourselves with distressed families, and even with police departments.

Patricia, for showing us the healing power of our presence when grieving people need to be heard.

Hal, for his generosity, kindness, and genius for heart-to-heart conversation.

Les, for finding common ground between all ages, cultures, and faiths with our stories.

Amy, for her amazing grace under pressure, showing us how art helps us to go with the flow, even in hectic times.

Pam, for her validation of our journeys, and for shining a light on the gifts of our journeys.

Don and Brenda and their dogs, for their unconditional love and acceptance.

Nancy and her horses, for their clarity, honesty, and firmness.

Laura and Whitney's Cherry Tree, for showing us the comfort of continuity, keeping rituals, and our reliability in showing up for each other's life passages.

Jen, for teaching us to take pause, to appreciate the radiance of stillness.

I thank more comforters of my life. My old friend Morna in Scotland across the ocean. My dear friends and family members in Virginia who have warmly and generously supported me. My newer friends in Maine, especially my friend Susan Neale, former publisher of the *Maine Women's Journal*, who first provided an opportunity for me to write profiles of comforting and courageous women. And all the readers and reviewers of my book in its many, many versions and stages.

The two wonderful people who guided, grounded, and encouraged me in bringing this book into the world: My editor at Tarcher/Penguin, Sara Carder, and my agent, Diane Freed.

My favorite writers and artists who have created the books, movies, music, and paintings that kept my spirit alive through the harsh winter and give me faith in the genius of all our hearts.

My beloved comforters in heaven, my cat Ivan, and my grandmother Viv.

And lunar moths, chickadees, and herons.

Comfort is all around me. I am never alone.

I step away from the water and turn toward the other side of the beach. There, glistening in the twilight on a rock, stands a magnificent blue heron, watching me closely. We behold each other for one moment, one that lives forever.

Index

Share *The Art of Comforting* with others

To order individual copies of this book, telephone Penguin Group USA Consumer Sales at 1-800-788-6262.

Most Penguin Group Books are available at special quantity discounts for bulk purchases for sales promotions, premiums, fund-raising, or educational use. Special books or book excerpts also can be created to fit specific needs.

Call PGI Special Markets for details on bulk quantity purchases. For *premiums, sales promotion, employee giveaways, fund-raisers,* or *reselling,* call 1-212-366-2612. Or write to Putnam Special Markets, 375 Hudson Street, New York, New York 10014.

Penguin's Business-to-Business (B2B) Advantage program allows your local bookseller to offer special discounted pricing for bulk sales. Your business, school, nonprofit, or church can receive special discounted pricing, great service, direct shipping, and more. Call your local bookstore and say you'd like to use Penguin's B2B program to buy your books for giveaway or training.

The Art of Comforting   978-1-58542-828-1 $15.95 ($20.00 CAN)

If you enjoyed this book, visit

www.tarcherbooks.com

and sign up for Tarcher's e-newsletter to receive
special offers, giveaway promotions, and
information on hot upcoming releases.

TARCHER
PENGUIN

Great Lives Begin with Great Ideas

New at **www.tarcherbooks.com**
and **www.penguin.com/tarchertalks**

Tarcher Talks, an online video series featuring
interviews with bestselling authors on everything from creativity and prosperity to 2012
and Freemasonry.

If you would like to place a bulk order
of this book, call 1-800-847-5515.